Viktoriia Grivina

Kharkiv—A War City
A Collection of Essays from 2022–2024

UKRAINIAN VOICES

Collected by Andreas Umland

72 *Pavlo Kazarin*
   Der Wilde Westen Ost-Europas
   Der ukrainische Weg aus dem Imperium
   Aus dem Ukrainischen übersetzt von Christian Weise
   ISBN 978-3-8382-1843-4

73 *Radomyr Mokryk*
   Die ukrainischen »Sechziger«
   Chronologie einer Revolte
   ISBN 978-3-8382-1873-1

74 *Leonid Finberg*
   My Ukraine
   Rethinking the Past, Building the Present
   ISBN 978-3-8382-1974-5

75 *Joseph Zissels*
   Consider My Inmost Thoughts
   Essays, Lectures, and Interviews on Ukrainian Matters at the Turn of the Century
   ISBN 978-3-8382-1975-2

76 *Margarita Yehorchenko, Iryna Berlyand, Ihor Vinokurov (eds.)*
   Jewish Addresses in Ukraine
   A Guide-Book
   With a foreword by Leonid Finberg
   ISB 978-3-8382-1976-9

The book series "Ukrainian Voices" publishes English- and German-language monographs, edited volumes, document collections, and anthologies of articles authored and composed by Ukrainian politicians, intellectuals, activists, officials, researchers, and diplomats. The series' aim is to introduce Western and other audiences to Ukrainian explorations, deliberations and interpretations of historic and current, domestic, and international affairs. The purpose of these books is to make non-Ukrainian readers familiar with how some prominent Ukrainians approach, view and assess their country's development and position in the world. The series was founded, and the volumes are collected by Andreas Umland, Dr. phil. (FU Berlin), Ph. D. (Cambridge), Associate Professor of Politics at the Kyiv-Mohyla Academy and an Analyst in the Stockholm Centre for Eastern European Studies at the Swedish Institute of International Affairs.

Viktoriia Grivina

KHARKIV—A WAR CITY
A Collection of Essays from 2022–2024

Bibliografische Information der Deutschen Nationalbibliothek
Die Deutsche Nationalbibliothek verzeichnet diese Publikation in der Deutschen Nationalbibliografie; detaillierte bibliografische Daten sind im Internet über http://dnb.d-nb.de abrufbar.

Bibliographic information published by the Deutsche Nationalbibliothek
The Deutsche Nationalbibliothek lists this publication in the Deutsche Nationalbibliografie; detailed bibliographic data are available on the Internet at http://dnb.d-nb.de.

Cover graphic: Illustration by Tetyana Pukhnavtseva

ISBN (Print): 978-3-8382-1988-2
ISBN (E-Book [PDF]): 978-3-8382-7988-6
© *ibidem*-Verlag, Hannover • Stuttgart 2025   Leuschnerstraße 40
                                                  30457 Hannover
                                                  Germany / Deutschland
Alle Rechte vorbehalten   info@ibidem.eu

Das Werk einschließlich aller seiner Teile ist urheberrechtlich geschützt. Jede Verwertung außerhalb der engen Grenzen des Urheberrechtsgesetzes ist ohne Zustimmung des Verlages unzulässig und strafbar. Dies gilt insbesondere für Vervielfältigungen, Übersetzungen, Mikroverfilmungen und elektronische Speicherformen sowie die Einspeicherung und Verarbeitung in elektronischen Systemen.

All rights reserved. No part of this publication may be reproduced, stored in or introduced into a retrieval system, or transmitted, in any form, or by any means (electronic, mechanical, photocopying, recording or otherwise) without the prior written permission of the publisher. Any person who commits any unauthorized act in relation to this publication may be liable to criminal prosecution and civil claims for damages.

Printed in the EU

To my parents, who brought me up in a free land,
and to great-grandma Oryna, who survived all that was before.

Content

Foreword 9

My Azov Sea 19

Kharkiv is My Home 29

Kyiv, not Kiev 37

A Visit to the Other City 43

What to Do with All the Russian Books 49

Merla, The River and the Goddess 59

Such a Warm, Such an Early April 65

I Watched Christopher Nolan's *Oppenheimer* in Ukraine:
His Greek Tragedy Is Our Reality 73

A City Big, But Not Great 77

In the Exploding Silence 85

Outro to "In the Exploding Silence" 101

Afterword 103

Acknowledgements 109

Foreword

This book was born out of sheer unadulterated hope. An eternal optimist, I could never have imagined that my beloved (and sometimes behated) hometown of Kharkiv could be attacked by a foreign army. Ever sleepy and nonchalant, its streets were meant to serve as the background for my imaginary fiction writings — sci-fi, detective and horror stories that would perfectly contrast the nothing-ever-happens-here vibe. Kharkiv was not supposed to become the stage of the most violent war in present-day Europe. It was not meant to become *a war city*. No city is meant to, for that matter. The time when it was fashionable to be an impregnable fortress has passed. Nor is it trendy to be called a "resilient hero city of the brave". Not that I'm against bravery and resilience, but I would rather do without.

In 2023, at a talk at Kharkiv National University, the director of the archaeological museum shared a story of a former student who joined the army and who, when inspecting abandoned Russian trenches, discovered an axe head that dated to the Bronze Age. Apparently, digging in, the Russian soldiers unintentionally entrenched themselves in a prehistoric camp. Russians didn't realize that they had uncovered an archaeological site. Fitting a wooden stick on the axe head, they used this priceless artifact as a meat cleaver in their field kitchen. During the liberation of the Kharkiv region in the fall of 2022, the fleeing Russian army took great care to take the most strategically important miliary necessities — washing machines, children's toys, a yellow boa constrictor from a private zoo, and so on. But the antique axe head, holding no value for them, was left behind in the field kitchen.

The former archaeology student sent the find to his alma mater in a simple Nova Post (a commonly used postal service) box, replenishing its collection, most of which had been evacuated. Learning that the Russians were using prehistoric tools in their attempt to colonize us made the museum visitors burst into laughter. We laughed as we passed the finding from hand to hand, touching an object normally kept behind protective glass, illuminated by specialized lighting in a temperature-controlled environment. Now it was not only a valuable exhibit, but one inscribed into our own life stories. The joke would become a legend, the legend a myth, and so on.

These lands, in which manuscripts were often burned and disappeared, are especially prone to mythmaking. Myths seep through the oily black earth of Kharkiv fields, saturating rich substrate of pain and blood with tales, jokes, and anecdotes. This is how Kharkiv preserves its memory. Through myths and a university student's find in the trenches. If we, Ukrainians, are wiped from the surface of the Earth, the oily black soil will whisper our stories from below.

Professional archaeologists, people who normally pass many seasons before finding an artifact worthy of a museum exhibit, are now fighting for Kharkiv. Through their double work, keeping watch over this city and the cities that came before, they not only have the chance to touch ancient history but to write a new one.

This is a story about knowledge. One has to know the land, the city, the village, the mill, respect local spirits and take on the responsibility for everyone and everything that can't be heard, all the people and objects that came before us, for the sake of all who will come after.

Kharkiv is a weird city, and it allows you to be weird with it. After Ukraine gained independence, a monument to a Russian writer at the entrance of the Kharkiv Central Park, Maksim Gorky, was replaced with a statue of a squirrel. A very logical choice, a local kid told me, since squirrels actually live in the park, and are almost universally adored, whereas Gorky never lived there, and is probably lying somewhere in a secret underground bunker, waiting to be resurrected for the next Russian project.

I've been trying to learn and respect the multiple weird his- and herstories of Kharkiv. The first thing to know is that it is a city on the northern border of the Wild Field. The Wild Field was a vast expanse of grassland and flowers that stretched between the north and south of Ukraine. It was cultivated and almost completely destroyed during the Soviet period. But, in our minds, we still live in this Wild Field.

Many legends float in the corner of the Wild Field where Kharkiv grew. The official year of the city's birth is 1654. Which is most likely untrue. The remains of three mythical cities can be found in the territory of present-day Kharkiv and its surrounding region. To the north, Saltiv conceals the remains of the culture of the Khazarian tribe.[1] Sharukan, the capital of a nomadic Polovtsian tribe that chased the Khazarians away, thrived somewhere along the Kharkiv River and further down the mighty Siverskyi Donets

---

1 Хлєсткова, Л. В. "Етнічна складова культурного простору Харкова." Гуманітарний часопис 2 (2006): 57-62.
Бубенок, О. Б., О. О. Хамрай, and В. В. Черноіваненко. "Монографія АЮ Кримського Історія хазарів з найдавніших часів до X віку"." Східний світ 3 (2011): 19-34.

River.[2] The Pechenihi, another nomadic people (squeezed somewhere between the Khazarians and the Polovtsians), gave their name to a township on the banks of Siverskyi Donets where my grandma was born.[3] Finally, the city of Donets itself—the legendary home of Sivertsi, an eastern Slavic tribe, known from Ihor's Song—was destroyed in the thirteenth century AD.[4] Its ruins lie in the territory of today's Kharkiv (making Kharkiv the real Donetsk: how about that for a plot twist?). Like the Pechenihi, Polovtsi, and Khazarians, the Sivertsy tribe came and built their city, saw it destroyed, and disappeared in the mists of time. However, some historians suggest that between the thirteenth and seventeenth centuries, some scattered settlements remained. And then, of course—long before anyone else—there were the Scythians, "our rich 'grandpas', the ones with all the gold and pyramids".

I often see Scythian burial mounds in the tender Ukrainian fields. The Scythian pyramids, kurgans—green hills suddenly rising amidst the trembling golden wheat—are protected by Ukrainian law. Destruction of Scythian burial sites can land you in prison. But if you are a pilot with the Russian strategic aviation units, of course, in which case your judgment day is far away, I'm afraid. It's funny that one tribe repurposed the leftovers of another. Polovtsians would make idols—babas—and place them on Scythian kurgan burial mounds, believing them their ancestors' graves. In the seventeenth century, Ukrainian Cossacks would halt their horses before the kurgans and pray to Jesus in front of Polovtsian babas, thinking both the babas and the graves belonged to their, i.e. our, ancestors. Despite the large crosses on their chests and a suspiciously fervent love of Jesus (but only the Orthodox one), many famous Cossacks, like Ivan Sirko (one of the probable founders of Kharkiv), liked to be seen as witchers (*"Kharakternyky"*). Witcher Cossacks possessed special powers and could see into the future. Legends floated around the Wild Field, about the brave Cossacks

---

2 Половець, Володимир Михайлович. "Половці: етнічна культура." (2012).
3 Танцюра, В. І., and О. Пересада. "Історія Слобідської України." ВІ Танцюра, ОО Пересада. Харків: ХНУ імені ВН Каразіна (2013).
4 Качало, С. І. "Прикордонна роль давньоруських пам'яток в басейні Сіверського Дінця." Праці Центру пам'яткознавства 26 (2014): 105-111.

who would lay a curse on the enemy's trail, assume the form of a gray wolf, or suddenly appear by a kurgan, praying to Polovtsian stone idols for victory.

If you haven't lost your way among all these many tribes, I applaud you. I still get mixed up in the tangled crowd of ghosts that surround me here. The lands of contemporary Kharkiv are teeming with peoples who gave this place its energy, spirit, memory, maybe even bits of DNA, which I notice in the warrior-like appearance of some locals. Remembering these ancient multitudes is our way of respecting this place, our home and theirs, even if archaeological sites raise more questions than answers as you dig in. Legends preserve our shared layered cultural DNA. My blood, which most likely has close to zero trace of those ancient lines, carries the stories of the mythical cities that came before my city, Kharkiv.

What Kharkiv was in the lean 1990s and lethargic 2000s, when I was growing up, scratching its surfaces with colored chalk, will never be forgotten and will never return. Perhaps, for the better even. Starting to write these essays in March 2022 I tried to preserve the elusive memory of the boring sun-drenched Kharkiv of my childhood. But also, to document how it felt to witness the city change so swiftly, so painfully, yet with so much hope.

One thing is certain — people always return here, to the confluence of the rivers Udy, Kharkiv and Lopan, and in this cozy nook legends are made. When I walk the streets of Kharkiv, the paths and dirt roads and high riverbanks, I feel spirits perch on my shoulder and whisper. To hear their fairy tales, you need quiet and focus. From time-to-time quiet sneaks in between the explosions. As the dust settles over ruined architecture, so unfairly slighted by the gaze of an international tourist, I try to uncover the past. This is when I listen to the old spirits with particular attention. The ghosts of this war, my friends and contemporaries, walk the streets too.

The Oldest Emblem of Kharkiv

And more discoveries continue to be made. In 2024 Oleh Dorozhenko, a historian turned soldier, was conducting research in the historical archive in Kyiv when he made an accidental discovery — the oldest emblem of Kharkiv, featured in the 1724 passport of a local who needed to travel to the nearby town of Chuhuiv.[5] The emblem shows a heart and a crown, along with a typical Cossack cross from the Baroque period.[6] Dorozhenko, who is now working on Ukrainian military history, states that these are common heraldic symbols of resilience, strength and honor. Today, though, the heart can also be seen as a symbol of love, vulnerability, kindness and empathy. The stories I include in this book are like that. The funny memories and naive reflections of a civilian who left Christ-

---

5   It's funny today to think that one needed a passport to travel from Kharkiv to Chuguiv, about as close to each other as London and Luton or Berlin and Brandenburg.
    Давидова, Юлія, Ємець, Валерія, "Серце, пронизане стрілами: історик знайшов у архівах ймовірний найдавніший герб Харкова, датований XVIII століттям", Suspilne, 16 June 2024.
6   When I speak of Cossacks, of course, I mean Ukrainian Cossacks.

masy boozy, party-going, carefree Kharkiv in January 2022 and returned in June 2022 to a beaten fighting cat of a city, its ears torn and bits of fur flying in the air.

I could not possibly write the thriller describing yesterday's baristas fighting alongside seasoned Ukrainian soldiers, firing on Russian tanks in early 2022 on a Kharkiv roundabout. These Ukrainian soldiers saved Kharkiv, my parents, everyone I love, and it's their story to tell. I cannot tell the story of Veronika Kozhushko, an eighteen-year-old artist killed by a Russian guided bomb on August 30, 2024. I used to see this stylish girl at various events hosted by Kharkiv's literary museum, sketching and being happy in the midst of this war, but we never got the chance to talk. On August 27, she sat next to me at a premiere of a Nafta Theatre play dedicated to the Ukrainian Executed Renaissance. Three days later she became our own executed Renaissance, a ghost in the crowd of friendly spirits. I'm sure that her friend, a talented writer, will tell the story of her beautiful life. I can't write the story of my dad driving the grandpa of my brother's wife to his school friend in the first days of the invasion, when it was very dangerous to get around. Or about this grandpa recalling the Nazi occupation of 1943 when some Hungarian officers took every piece of furniture out of their flat, leaving only a piano because a German officer who lodged himself there liked to play it. These are someone else's fascinating, chilling, infinitely more important tales. What I have written about here are small anecdotes, bits and bobs of life, the funny and sad things that I saw myself, what I felt living in Kharkiv, experiencing the good, the bad and the deadly days in the optimistic delusion that the good must win and the "baddies", as my British friends say, — must lose.

I often think of an episode of the Doctor Who series called "Don't Blink". It revolves around aliens who pose as statues in a city and steal human time when their victims turn away. There is a moment in this episode when the heroine meets a young police detective. As they search an abandoned house, it starts to rain. The detective is caught by the statues and sent into the past. By the time the rain ends, the heroine receives a call from the hospital where the policeman is dying of old age. War steals time in a similar way. One day in 2022 I woke up from a very beautiful dream. Making breakfast, I was walking around the kitchen smiling, singing under my breath. It was the first time since 2014 that I had seen Crimea, even if it was only a dream.

I started working on this essay in September 2021, months before the big war, and finished it in May 2022, months into it. In that seemingly short stretch of time, the main hero of my text, the Azov Sea, was captured and occupied by the Russian army. The thin line of the Arabat Spit, which separates the Azov from a salty wetlands of the Syvash, has become unreachable, and my holiday spent on its endless shallow beaches the autumn before its occupation a painful memory of stolen time. This immense, invisible gap of time bleeds through the text, slowly crawling to the spot where the cut occurs. The alien invasion is not explicitly shown; rather omitted, which makes the words slightly fragile and imperfect around the edges of the wound. Yet this is exactly what my body experiences, imperfection and fragility, in these times when I cannot stand in front of the Russian tanks and protect my childhood memories from the piercing gaze of war.

I feel that when I see Crimea and my Azov Sea next time, I will be very, very old, because the world always gets worse before it gets better. I saw it all in that good dream of mine. Besides, some of my treasures are still hidden on a mount overlooking Ayu-Dag. And Ukrainians never abandon their treasures!

My Azov Sea[7]

In the early autumn of 2021, I repeated my old childhood route from Kharkiv to the sea of Azov. There, in the lazy silence of Schastlyvtseve (The Lucky Village) as the holiday season was rolling to its close, I felt a tremendous moment of quiet before the storm.

September sea along the thin land strip of the Arabat spit was quiet and cold. My friend and I came on a bus at dawn, and, surrounded by a pack of stray and strangely menacing huskies (the most bizarre Stephen Kingian sort of danger I'd ever experienced), walked to the white ribbon of the beach. The Spit with its longest, but not necessarily cleanest, beach in Europe is covered in crushed shells, "rakushnyak." Rakushnyak is ever present. Houses are built out of it, the ground is made of it, and my hair and lungs instantly filled with it too. The Spit stretches all the way to Crimea. In 2014, the Russians, exercising the privilege of force and terror over the international community, occupied not only Crimea, but half of the Spit too. An elderly couple in the bus on our way here had asked the driver if they would be able to cross to "the Russian side." The driver gave them the quiet understanding gaze of a psychiatrist faced with a curious case, and agreed to drop the couple off at the last village on the Spit. An additional payment of fifty hryvnias was duly made.

The Arabat Spit, also known as the Strelka ("arrow"), cuts the Azov from the Syvash, a chain of shallow lagoons, filled with salt and all kinds of marine life: small bychki ("little bulls", bony fish), iglas ("needles", pipefish) and tiny local shrimps, good enough when boiled with dill and an herb called soleros (salicornia). Everything is not what it seems: bychky are not bulls, iglas aren't needles, and the shrimps are nothing like those in a supermarket. Soleros is the only thing that is what it is. "Sol" means salt, and "ros" means to grow. Like the crushed shells, *soleros* grows everywhere from Azov to the salty meadows of the Syvash. You can taste

---

7   *Tint Journal* (Fall 2022), https://tintjournal.com/essay/my-azov-sea.

it at a local fine dining restaurant, with balsamic vinegar and German Riesling. Or pick for free on the beach after swimming in the shallow Azov, then add to your tomato salad.

Growing up I spent every summer here with my grandpa, whom the Komsomolsk power plant rewarded with a seasonal managerial position at the plant's holiday house. No one in our family knew what grandpa did as an employee of the power plant for the rest of the year, since the only qualification we knew he had was a teacher of arts and crafts. Such were the Ukrainian 1990s, filled with wonder and a salary payments in the form of Earl Grey tea, which grandpa once extracted from the plant, and made my dad drink it for a year despite my dad's ingrained dislike of bergamot.

The road from Kharkiv was a 10-hour adventure, wrapped in boiling heat, smell of corn, freshwater crabs and chibereki (thin fried Tatar meat pies), which every passenger felt the urge to buy at the roadside markets you could recognize from afar by the beach towels swaying in the wind. A tiger, a naked lady and a dollar sign were the three most popular patterns on the towels. On the road back, somewhere around Novomoskovsk, well-rested workers of the power plant would also buy sets of painted enamel bowls, courtesy of the local enamel factory workers and their businesses on the side. Because grandpa always shook hands with the right people, I could enjoy this adventure for free. In Komsomolsk my mom would put me on an overturned crate next to the driver, and on Azov grandpa would be waiting with a gigantic Kherson watermelon, to buy me out. I felt like one of those Cossacks who got captured and returned from the Istanbul slave traders after their families would pay the arranged price.

My wild summer would start then and there, melting in the sweet syrup of melons and peaches, the buzz of mosquitoes and the ever-lasting boredom of Azov. Unlike Crimea, which had always been too expensive for an honest family like ours, the Spit did not have much to offer to a wandering eye. It was just an endless beach with a lonely tree by the road, a herd of cows and an occasional farmer's plane ("*kukuruznik*") that sprinkled sun-bathers with mosquito poison. To my dad it was perfect. The most he'd spend would be a couple of hryvnias for my paprika crisps and strawberry cornetto ice cream.

We'd waste time playing blackjack on the beach, using shells for money, and catching shrimps on the Syvash with the lace curtain we'd take off the window in grandpa's hotel room. Once a week we'd go "to the city" of Henichesk, and buy a huge meaty Pelengas fish (redlip mullet) to cook on a barbecue with herbs and baby potatoes. And every evening I'd see (for free, courtesy of grandpa's connections) the two films our hotel cinema owned — *The Lion King* and *Ace Ventura*. I knew them by heart.

My dad would sometimes drive from work for a weekend and take us to Crimea in his old Soviet white car. We'd go through the Spit and all along the southern coast to Yalta and Alupka's Vorontsov palace. I could hardly believe my eyes, thinking that these mountains and beaches were "mine". During my teenage years my rebellion was to abandon Azov for Crimea and hike with the Kharkiv Polytechnic tourist club, sleeping in tents on the wild beaches, drinking sweet Massandra wine and jumping into the deep Black Sea from the rocks. Another impossible thing on the shallow shores of Azov.

I never got to visit the main Crimean festivals, the notorious Kazantip, or the more cultured Koktebel Jazz. That felt like something you could always do later. Like Donetsk or Luhansk. After 2014 Koktebel Jazz lost its home base of, well, Koktebel, and became a nomadic on-and-off event. And now in 2021 it was advertised as the last musical happening of the holiday season.

My friend, who had been to the real Koktebel Jazz, was disillusioned already when we jumped off the bus. The first thing she noted was that there was no music coming from anywhere. Everything but the wild husky pack seemed to sleep. We walked through the wind, squinting at the rising sun, and called our Airbnb host. A tall quiet woman in a beige headscarf greeted us by the tall gates. She didn't mind us arriving five hours early, as we seemed to be the only tourists around. Having showed us the room, she walked off to the beach with her kids. I didn't need to ask to know our hosts were Crimean Tatars. It wasn't just the headscarf. Only those who've lost a sea once can appreciate it.

Back in Crimea — before 2014, when it was still mine — I once stayed in another former Tatar house. My host was an old Russian woman whose husband had worked in a mine in Donbas, and received the house as a thank you from the Soviet government. After 1944 the peninsula was subjected to massive resettlement, where you mostly had to be ethnically Russian to have the right to move in. Ukrainians weren't welcome, though, also not persecuted for visiting. Unlike the Krymchaks (one of the names of Crimean Tatars) who were banned from the peninsula until 1989. The house was situated right on the territory of the national park, and I stayed in a wing, built apparently for the household animals, but still sturdy enough. The well in the garden was dry — not many of the Russian settlers knew how to take care of natural springs as they would often come from very different landscapes, therefore the situation with water in Crimea had been slowly deteriorating since 1940s. I would always get "second-day food poisoning", a reward for forgetting not to cook with water from the tap. When asked, my elderly host preferred to keep silent about the original owners of the house. Soviet people, instructed by the system, never liked the Krymchaks. I often wondered afterwards if, like many, she'd met the descendants of the owners, if they ever knocked at her door in the 1990s, showing old photographs, asking to look around. Soviet settlers tended to treat Tatars with aggression coming, very understandably, from guilt.

In Shastlivtseve our hosts' house, pool and a chain of motel-like rooms were clean and freshly painted. Only poisonous spiders that we brought in the bouquets of wildflowers would sometimes pop up in my bed, making me scream in surprise.

Koktebel Jazz was a pale shadow of its normal self, my friend would admit. The holiday season over, trucks with ice cream and cold beer were shutting down, and the evening shows on the beach featured three moderately drunk men in their fifties feeding cats on an empty dance floor by the stage. Algae, wind and seagulls were taking over the vast emptiness for the winter. On the second day of the festival we walked to the Pink Lake instead. A family looking for the lake picked us up, even though we weren't hitchhiking specifically. "We all here need to help each other", the father at the driving seat said. He used to spend summers in Crimea as a child. Now Azov had become the main destination for his three kids.

Driving back from the Spit a day later, I looked at the Syvash lagoon, trying to imagine how salt merchants of the eighteenth century, "*chumaks*", dried salt along the coast, and undertook dangerous summer treks through the wild steppes, teeming with nomadic criminal bands, to sell salt and bring prosperity to their villages. There's a town called Valky in my region — named after a cart filled with *chumak* salt.

I was coming back to Kharkiv with bouquets of *soleros* instead. Azov was quiet, sleepy, ready for the winter, as if my last look at its waters sealed it for the next time. But also, somehow, the atmosphere was alert, somehow irrationally nervous. The feeling that half of the Spit was occupied, and that there, after a certain line we used to drive through every summer, now Russian soldiers stood their guard, brought ominous thoughts. As if I could hear those soldiers speak between one another in the distance. I lay sleepless during the nights, listening to the dark.

A friend who was driving from the Black Sea picked us up in Melitopol on the way back. Like mine, her stories were both cheerful, a surfing weekend, and sad — stories of persecuted Crimeans she was working with. We stopped by the museum of Melitopol, a beautiful 1913 mansion hidden behind white poplars. We walked around the garden and the collection of Scythian gold. Our guide said they'd won a Ukrainian Cultural Fund Grant and were expecting restorations to begin. The gold has now been looted and, as in ancient times, taken to the center of the empire, with the director Leila Ibragimova kidnapped. I don't know if it has to do with Leila being Crimean. But I'm grateful that I saw this island of southern Ukrainian culture before, even if I know I'll see it again.

It was a strange feeling, of hope and silence, when we returned to the highway. I did not want to abandon it. As if, in leaving, we were calling for winter to come. A sign showed the Stone Grave national reserve on the right. Our friend said she had always wanted to have a look. Why not, we answered, and drove into the hot steppes of Zaporizhia. The Stone Grave is a natural arrangement of large stones used for thousands of years by a variety of tribes for rituals and other unknown purposes. The natural reserve is a sandy terrain, and many Scythian and Polovets idols, called babas, were brought here from surrounding ancient burial sites or kurgans. Kurgans pop up in the steppes from the Black Sea all the way to Kharkiv. Ukrainian warrior Cossacks considered them the graves of their ancestors and stopped to pray to babas. Today these idols are under government protection. Walking along the Stone Grave I felt like an actor in a *Star Wars* movie. It was a space-like kind of landscape. Tiny vipers skirted gravel paths under my feet. But I wasn't scared. There are places where rationale halts.

There are such times too. I dreamt of the Stone Grave for a week before the new Russian invasion began. In my dreams I walked between the stones, and the Sea of Azov, like an overturned mirror, looked at me from above.

In February the Russian army occupied the Spit, bizarrely erecting a statue of Lenin in Henichesk. The last thing I heard about the village of Shastlivtseve was that someone tore down the Russian flag from the village council and put the Ukrainian one back. The news was shared by the Crimean Tatar Facebook community.

Every day the war was stepping closer — I read about the ancient Stone Grave in the news in March, a missile fell into the debris of the sandy ground. The lands around the Grave have been now covered in Russian mines. The Melitopol museum was looted and bombed.

The war stepped closer — to my home region of Kharkiv, which I returned to on that late and hot September. The war came to the stone babas on Mount Kremenets, their empty eyes overlooking the town of Izium down in the valley. The house of my cousin's aunt stands there as silent as the emptiness we hear in the receiver when trying to dial familiar numbers — we haven't heard from them since March 2.

The war came closer — to the old Ukrainian fortress of Chuguiv, the home of "a famous Russian painter" Illya Repin, who grew up enchanted with old Cossack folklore, painting churches along the tall grassy banks of the Donets River. On February 24 one of the first Russian missiles hit the Aviator district, and my other cousins bundled their children into the car and drove through a night filled with sirens and fire, never looking back.

The war came closer — to the "East Village" on the outskirts of Kharkiv, to the house where I grew up, when my parents called and, trying not to sound alarmed, mentioned that a missile landed on the driveway behind their car, and that chipped glass from nearby windows littered the fresh layer of their recently renovated tarmac.

It then broke into central Kharkiv, to the crossroads of Science Avenue and Culture Street, the street where *Slovo*, the Ukrainian writers' house was shelled. A couple of streets from where I'd been dropped off in early September 2021, carrying a bouquet of *soleros* and an enormous Kherson watermelon in a tote bag. The war came to the apartment where I'd walked into after my trip to Azov. The apartment where that warm September night we ate the watermelon with prosecco, and where the bouquet of *soleros* still hangs from a nail on a balcony. Volunteers lived there, and now it is empty, as my friends and I are trying to assemble our lives elsewhere, in the hope that we will return.

The war came into my body on February 24, when I started trembling and never stopped, and still, sometimes, shake suddenly, and objects fall out of my hands. I sit on the floor and let myself shake every once in a while, like a stalk of soleros, waiting for the land to stabilize. It happens when Kharkiv is being shelled, and my dad won't answer the phone. I wake up from explosions in my dreams, or a message of another bombed museum. I wake up and try to find news about Henichesk, the occupied Arabat Spit, about the kind and thoughtful Crimean Tatars who liked to walk to the beach in the morning. It's not a flashy topic. I now return to Azov in my mind, and miss its beautiful boredom. Among the fears of its extinction, the mines and the disappearing soleros, I want to know there is a place that looks exactly like it was yesterday when my grandpa bought me out with that legendary Kherson watermelon.

***

More on Crimean Tatars:

1. The Crimean Tatar Resource Center, https://www.freiheit.org/ost-und-sudosteuropa/crimean-tatar-resource-center
2. Eve Conant, "Behind the Headlines: Who Are the Crimean Tatars?", *National Geographic News,* last modified March 15, 2014, https://www.nationalgeographic.com/history/article/140314-crimea-tatars-referendum-russia-muslim-ethnic-history-culture

Kharkiv is My Home *was published in the morning of April 4, 2022, when the first photographs from the just liberated Bucha started to appear on the screen of my phone. I was still in bed, the window of the room overlooking a serene Scottish garden with a giant tree, a reminder of Celts and ancient battles. It was my birthday. It was probably the worst day of my life (so far, of course, no illusions here). It was the day when the old and rusty word "genocide" started to make its way through the waters of history back into Ukraine. Both Babyn Yar and Drobytsky Yar — the sites of the mass murder of Jewish people in World War II — were shelled along with many homes around. First introduced by Raphael Lemkin (who studied in Lviv, a fact that we very proudly push in everyone's face), "genocide" is not a word you want to use when talking about your people. It's an uncomfortable word. Overused, compromised, definitely not cool. I could not pronounce this word, partly because I pretend that I don't have the habit of talking to myself, and partly because it actually sounds obscene. This word made the nature of the war uncomfortable, and our stake in it infinitely high. Before leaving the serene Scottish house that morning, I took a picture of myself in the mirror just to make sure that I was alive. The published article, haphazard and fragmentary, jumping from thought to thought, is not unlike that sudden selfie. Submitted to the Vietnamese magazine Saigoneer to make sure that somewhere on the other side of the globe, in a land I've never seen, a mark, a scratch would be left of the fact that my friends and I lived, that we existed, and that all of it happened precisely to us.*

Kharkiv is My Home[8]

On February 24, I couldn't fall asleep. In the middle of the night my phone lit up and a message from my friend appeared, "It was the right thing to worry". Another friend wrote, "Explosions". I tried to refresh the page of *Hromadske*, a popular Ukrainian news outlet, but most Ukrainian news websites were attacked by Russian hackers the moment our cities were attacked by Russian bombs. Explosions woke up every one of my friends in Kharkiv, Kyiv, and all across Ukraine. I went to a local social media channel that normally posted jokes and pictures of bizarre-looking people on the metro.

"Kharkiv is being bombed. The airport in Chuguiv destroyed. Explosions in the center", the site wrote. The message was followed by a meme about Russian bots flooding the channel and a note that comments would be closed for that reason. In those early hours, my body started to shake, even though I was far away, beginning my PhD in Scotland. A month later, this strange trembling still continues. Two sentences ago, my hands were trembling; now it has stopped.

I called my dad's number, our home number, but to no response. The official channel of our mayor said, "Please refrain from leaving your homes today". When I finally reached my dad at around 8 a.m., he said: "Oh, I've decided to go to work". For my dad the war was not a reason grave enough to skip his routines. On his way he saw many Kharkivians spilling into the streets, looking around their apartment buildings, confused; they talked to their neighbors and directed various curses to Belgorod, a nearby city in Russia from which the bombs and missiles came.

That was another first for Ukrainians: the experience of sheer hatred and fury. February in Ukrainian translates literally as "furious". If fury was fuel, Ukrainians would be the world's richest energy producer today. Kharkiv might have been one of the most furious, and thus richest, cities in Ukraine.

---

8   *Saigoneer*, April 4, 2022, https://saigoneer.com/news/21025-letter-from-ukra ine-kharkiv-is-my-home,-i-never-imagine-that-we-could-be-attacked

With a population of over 1.6 million, Kharkiv is filled with students, IT industry, and nuclear physics. It's also the home of the biggest producer of instant noodles, Mivina, brought to us by the Vietnamese businessman Phạm Nhật Vượng back in 1995. Mivina are the noodles that we used to eat at school breaks like crisps after smashing an unopened pack; they defined our poor but free existence. We thankfully never knew the Soviet Union, and always did whatever we wanted as kids.

Kharkiv is my home. Leaving for St. Andrews University from the shiny Kharkiv airport, in the reflections of bright sun against the snow, I didn't cry. I was confident the airport would still be there when I go back in May. I could never imagine that the city could be attacked. The last time any military action took place in Kharkiv was 1943. Now I'm seeing the old World War II photos come alive. I see the war through the eyes of my friends and family.

Nadya, my best friend from school, co-owns a trendy Asian fusion restaurant called GaGa. She sent me that first message. Like many Kharkivians, Nadya did not believe the full-scale invasion was happening. The night the bombing started, she didn't even have her documents packed. She spent the first hours cleaning her apartment, where I had also lived just a month before. It's located in a university area that's very central and full of international students, with parks and coffee shops, hip bars and a vibrant nightlife.

Many university buildings would be destroyed in the days to come, as the Russian military started looking for the biolabs falsely being reported on Russian news. On that first day, Nadya went to hide in the metro. Foreigners often wonder why Kharkiv underground platforms are so spacious. In fact, they were constructed as possible bomb shelters, the safest places in the city. But Nadya soon got cold and went to the Yermilov Contemporary Art Centre, a gallery situated in the cellars of the National University. This space also hosted Pavlo Makov, an artist whose *Fountain of Exhaustion* will be presented in the Ukrainian pavilion at the upcoming Venice Biennale.

To be inert is not something that Nadya is capable of, so after two days, she returned to GaGa with her team to start cooking for our military, the territorial defense forces, for hospitals, and for people hiding in the metro. Several days later, the square next to GaGa was bombed. The cafe's window was damaged, and the team decided to move to a smaller town away from the bombings where they were offered a bigger kitchen. Today, they are cooking over 3,000 meals a day for Kharkivians and are driving back and forth hundreds of kilometers to deliver the meals.

Another friend, Nastya, lives just a couple of streets away from Nadya. She spent the first days of the invasion in a bomb shelter under her house with her mom, three cats she recently adopted, and a group of international medical students from India, Turkey and the United Arab Emirates. She admired them for fixing the lights and creating comfort in the shelter by bringing carpets and furniture. For some, it wasn't the first war by far.

After the students were evacuated several days later, Nastya started looking after four more cats that students left behind, hoping one day to return. She reopened her Etsy-only shop to post an option for donations, as she feared that it could become harder to feed everyone, though students are also trying to help from abroad. She is an optimist, even though we exchange some of the most heartbreaking messages:

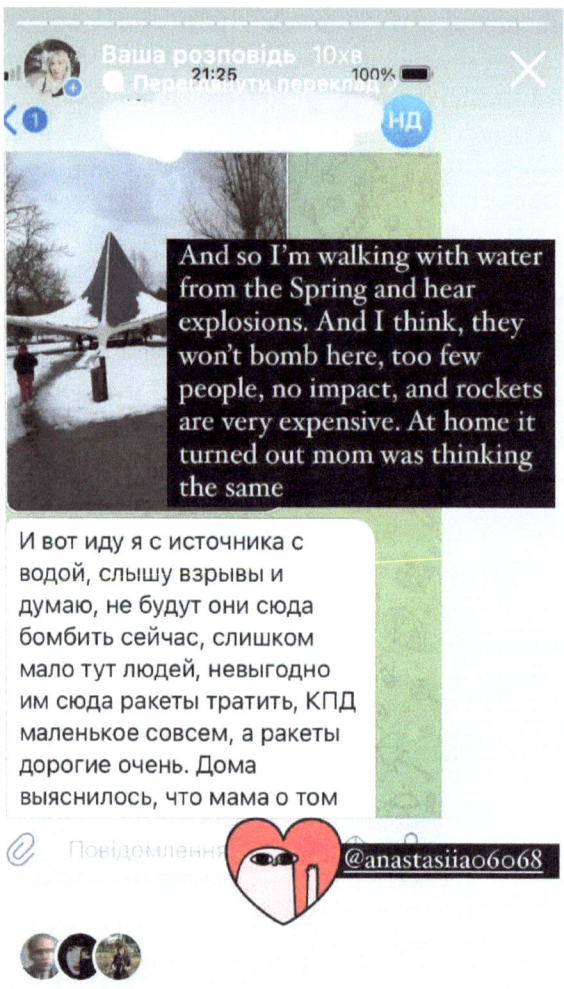

A message from Nastya.

Most of my friends left Kharkiv—some on the first night, with a variety of adventures that deserve a book of their own. My parents stayed, though I am still asking them to leave. However, today's roads can be as dangerous as the bombs, with Russian soldiers going mad from hunger and anger. They have shot several people that we know already. Kharkiv has to stand. There is no other option.

I watched the city through the eyes of famous Kharkivians like Serhii Zhadan, a Ukrainian poet and writer. Not only did he stay, but he continues to document life, organize concerts and provide help across the city. In his eyes, Kharkiv is alive, even if wounded, filled with volunteers, freedom and hope. He has been nominated for this year's Nobel prize by the Polish Academy of Science.

Another friend of mine, a young artist named Olia Fedorova, has become a media celebrity because of her choice to stay. She started a diary on social media, reporting her life under bombardment and organizing guitar concerts with her neighbors. Olia's partner joined the territorial defense, though it took him three attempts, as the lines in front of recruitment offices were especially long in the first days.

Finally, we have a four-paw hero. In the face of horrific stories like the bombed zoo and Feldman ecopark where volunteers lost their lives rescuing animals, one uplifting story has captured everyone's attention. Stepan, a famous TikTok cat who lives in the heavily shelled Saltivka District, disappeared from social media for a while. People were alarmed, as Stepan and his lazy poses by enormous glasses of exotic drinks symbolized the chill spirit of Kharkiv. He returned in the third week of the war, reporting his hardships fleeing the city and getting across the Polish border to be rescued by an association of influencers. He became a champion for helping Ukrainian animals.

As of today, more than 600,000 people have left Kharkiv. Local authorities are now asking civilians to leave and not risk their lives. All Kharkivians I know plan to return when the city is safe again. I am no exception. I have decided to return, either after victory, or when I feel that I will be needed to defend the city.

The famous Ukrainian linguist and writer Yury Shevelov, a Kharkivian himself, once wrote an essay, "The Fourth Kharkiv", revealing the history of the city, as though it went through a process of shedding skin like a snake. It was originally built as a fortress for Ukrainian warriors—Cossacks. Under the Russian Empire, it was reduced to a provincial town, then the university appeared, and Kharkiv became a hotbed of Ukrainian nationalism through the nineteenth century, and the first capital of Soviet Ukraine in the 1920s.

During Stalin's rule, it was a place of tragedy. Many Ukrainian intellectuals were exterminated and Ukrainian farmers died of the imposed famine, called the Holodomor. The loss of the Executed Renaissance—artists and writers who died for being Ukrainian in the 1930s—led to the city slowly freezing into a gray and unimportant Soviet town. Shevelov had to flee to the US, but predicted that a Fifth Kharkiv would emerge—a new stronghold.

Kharkiv is a proud city, a jewel of the Ukrainian East with a two-hundred-year-old university, my alma mater, and hundreds of thousands of talented, tech-savvy young people. It was built as a fortress against nomadic conquerors from the south. Today it is once again a fortress that stands against invaders from the north. If Ukraine stands, Kharkiv, even wounded and hurting, has a bright future ahead.

If any of my Kharkiv friends suspected that a text entitled Kyiv, Not Kiev would end up in a KHARKIV book, they'd make me swear on parks, benches, and the famous Buffet square pizza to stop the blasphemy. And yet, here it is, and you, dear reader, know the consequences I will face for it.

In the first months of the big war, I took on the heavy burden (nobody asked me to take) of telling fellow students about Ukraine. Organizing tiny reading groups, where poor Russophiles had to wrap their heads around the other Cyrillic, was a fun way to see how easy it appeared for the undergrads to soak in the complexities of Vasyl Stus, or the tender romanticism of Lesya Ukrainka. At the same time, at conferences, I found it almost impossible to explain to some important academics the simplest rules, such as how the names of Ukrainian cities should be written and why it is so important for us that Ukrainian cities be spelled according to the Ukrainian transcription. Russophone professors would come to me and try to speak in Russian, and not understand why I, "a student from Kharkiv", would insist on speaking English instead of the language in which they were comfortable and which they knew that I knew. For years they'd been taught in their Russian courses that Kharkiv and the rest of the "near abroad" was supposed to be devotedly Russophone. They couldn't grasp why I refused to meet on their turf, suspecting I had some sort of a jaw condition. Translator by my first MA, I'd never had to translate my own country so relentlessly for other people as after the full-scale war began. This constant extra work, though mostly invigorating, has been taking much strength. I'm sure other Ukrainians are facing the same addition to their lives. This essay came out of a duality, a strange duality, where back home things would be constantly and drastically changing, while here, in the comfortable West, nothing changed.

For some we are still part of the Soviet sphere of influence, and the shadow of communism, in the figure of a Lenin's bald head, is preventing us from becoming fully visible. But one thing makes me hopeful. On Klochkivska Street in Kharkiv there is an old car repair store. In the yard of this store there lie dozens of Lenin's heads, which the owner had been collecting for years. He'd drive around the villages and ask local heads (all pun intended) if they would give up a Lenin, long before any decommunization laws. Lenins flanked the shop, staring at passers-by through a rusty metal fence with the word "СТЕКЛО" written on it. Jailed between a church and a new hotel complex, the lenins await their Valhalla, suffering the sights of a blooming Ukrainian capitalism. As you can see, we are extremely experienced at slaying dragon heads.

Kyiv, not Kiev[9]

The life of a Ukrainian PhD student doing cultural studies at St. Andrews, like anywhere abroad, is complicated, complex, and nuanced. My first MA was in the English and German languages and translation at Kharkiv University. I have now become a translator from the language of war. A couple of times every week I get to write or say one of the following phrases: "It's Kyiv, not Kiev", "It's Ukraine, not the Ukraine", "It's democratic, not post-Soviet". I say these words with a mixture of gratitude, for people have started to listen to me, and sadness, for if it were public knowledge, I could have used my time better, explaining how Ukrainian culture has become like a rhizome — a network of horizontal connections that can never be fully destroyed or uprooted. About the last Yiddish writer Joseph Burg from Chernivtsi, or Bruno Schultz from Drohobych, or Mykola Khvylovy, the Ukrainian Joyce. "Kyiv, not Kiev" is about the language. In Ukrainian it's "Київ", making it "Kyiv" in Latin letters. Until 1991 we did not have our own state, but were a colony of the Russian and Austro-Hungarian empires, and then of the Soviet Union. We were named in the languages of these empires: in German, Lemberg, or in Polish, Lwow. Between 1939 and 1991 our entire territory was part of the Soviet Union, and so our cities were written in Russian — Kiev, Kharkov, Odessa, Lvov. Our own language did not have the right to international representation. The Ukrainian language is a survivor, however. It survived more than 150 bans during the Russian empire alone. The Ukrainian typeface was prohibited. Papers, theaters, and universities would be closed for using Ukrainian. Poets like Taras Shevchenko or Vasyl Stus were imprisoned, others like Vasyl Symonenko killed. Yet others like Mykola Gogol or Anton Chekhov changed their identities as a survival strategy and were appropriated by the empire. Like Malevich, Delone, Bohomazov, and many more. Ukrainian culture grew in the cracks between the concrete of

---

9   "Kyiv, not Kiev: Translating from War", *St. Leonard's College Magazine*, 2023.

Russian and Soviet domination. Whispered, not shouted; revolutionary songs sung behind closed doors, while Big Brother wasn't listening. Like it was in my family and my friends' families with the songs of the anarchist Batko Makhno. "Where are you now, the torturers of my people?" — Vasyl Symonenko asked this before he was killed in 1963. I often recite his poem in my head. Symonenko writes about a Ukrainian's "sharp and tender soul", hardened by centuries of fighting. And now, my soul is sharp and hardened. One part is constantly in Ukraine, reading news, calling loved ones after every bomb dropped on my city of Kharkiv. St. Andrews can't see me as a whole person, because half is always not here. Being only half of my usual self-complicates building friendships, and I feel much lonelier than I did during my Master's here in 2019-2020. At the same time, I feel part of a bigger society, tragic and fascinating. When you don't have your own state, a poem, a song, an image become the saviors of your people. Such was "the Ukraine", a piece of land between empires, a stateless nation that survived by hiding its treasures or presenting them jokingly as a shield. The first lecture in Ukrainian was presented at Kharkiv University as a "joke, a bet to prove that serious things can be said in Ukrainian". Hryhory Kvitka wrote his romantic novel *Marusia* in 1834 as another bet to prove to a Russian acquaintance that dramatic texts could be written in "the low people's language". A story familiar to Mary Shelley, whose *Frankenstein* was also born of a light-hearted bet against the ruling sex. Indeed, Ukrainian literature has been very open to women writers of various ethnicities. From the German-speaking Olha Kobylianska, our main early twentieth-century feminist, author of the novel *Lyudyna* ("A Human" — in Ukrainian, this word is feminine), to an ethnic Russian, Maria Vilinska, who in a very George Sand sort of way became a male Ukrainian writer, Marko Vovchok (Marco the Wolf). Ivan Franko used to say that Lesia Ukrainka was the only real man in the entirety of Ukrainian literature. Post-Soviet? Imagine calling German people post-Nazi in daily conversation. Soviet rule killed more Ukrainians than the Nazi one, granted the Soviets had more time. European? Nuanced? Complex? Counterintuitively, Ukrainian culture is fundamentally different from that of its Eastern and Western neighbors. Russian literature is blunt, in your face, filled with epic panoramas. Tolstoy's Europe consists of three states—Russia, Germany and France—which is how the Russian army travels in *War and Peace*, ending up at a ball in a provincial Russian town of Vilno (Lithuanian Vilnius), celebrated as liberators (the Lithuanians who were conquered by Russians at that moment left a very different account of the Russian army, of course).[10] Ukrainian Europe consists of a myriad of ethnicities, minorities, neighbors and opponents, local dialects and tastes, one in which Hungarians were called "Madiary", because that is what they call themselves, where Lemkos were an important part of culture even before one of them became Andy Warhol. Ivan Kotsiubynsky traveled to the Carpathians to learn about Hutsuls, the mountain folk, and wrote a tragic love story about a Hutsul boy and girl. Fifty years later an Armenian-Ukrainian director, Serhii Paradjanov, undertook the same route to make a poetically beautiful film adaptation of the story, *Shadows of Forgotten Ancestors*. This mutual interest in differences and details make Ukrainian literature and film stand out. Ivan Franko wrote a poem, "Kamenyary" (which translates as "Stonemasons") where a group of unknown heroes chisel a path through the mountain so that "the future free generations could walk upon our bones along the road that we make", "even if we ourselves are forgotten by everyone". It is true: Europe forgot Ivan Franko, and Lesya Ukrainka. Walking into a bookshop in St. Andrews I won't find books by Vasyl Symonenko, Vasyl Stus, Mykola Khvylyovy, Maik Johanssen, Mikhailo Semenko, Pavlo Tychyna, Volodymyr Sosyura, Taras Shevchenko or Panas Myrny, Ivan Bahrany, and many more. But there I am, a person for whom Ivan Franko wrote his "Stonemasons". The first generation of the free people. I think of Ivan Franko often; I think that he wrote these lines to me. I walk the road that he and other forgotten heroes chiseled in the concrete mountain of these bloody empires. I walk on the bones of brave unrecognized giants. And this is why I will never get tired of saying: It's Kyiv, not Kiev. It's Ukraine, the biggest democratic state in Europe.

---

10 Thompson, Ewa M. (Ewa Majewska), Imperial Knowledge: Russian Literature and Colonialism / Ewa M. Thompson. (Greenwood Press, 2000)

It will never be "the Ukraine" again. Its culture is complex and nuanced. Western academia will grow to know and love this culture if it gives this culture a chance.

When I was helping to organize a residency for artists and writers in the bed of the Carpathian Mountains in June 2022, the serene little town of Vyzhnytsia where we were staying was still full of internally displaced families. Most of them had very little idea of their future, lost and confused. Mothers volunteered at a local cinema that was by day converted into humanitarian aid point. Secondhand clothes collected from all over Europe were festively spread over the cinema seats, and our resident artists would choose the most bizarre acid green and leather pieces to parade around the town, as if they had come straight from a Berlin rave. The refugees themselves already full of European clothes and food, were more interested in the workshops and film screenings, walking tours and museum visits. Desperately looking for something to do, young mothers came round with their kids, to chat and loosen the terrible glue of monotonous days. Many of these families were from Mariupol and Kharkiv and treated these cities as equally unreal.

On a bus trip to the village of Kryvorivnia, where the magical Shadows of Forgotten Ancestors was filmed, a young woman with a little boy started to chat. She said suddenly, "We are from Kharkiv, refugees, and you?". "I'm from Kharkiv too. But I'm not a refugee", I answered, and immediately an awkward pause materialized. It was so strange that here I was, fresh from the city I would come back to after this trip. And there they were, people who had lost their city forever. My Kharkiv, with its cafés and parks, and sushi takeaway, was just two days from here. And their Kharkiv, dead and gone, was there in the woman's weary eyes. And we stood blinking at each other, a refugee and a non-refugee of Kharkiv. In identical multicolored T-shirts, courtesy of Berlin ravers' European humanitarian aid.

A Visit to the Other City[11]

I've recently been told about the novel *Unterstadt*, in which the Croatian author Ivana Šojat writes about returning to her hometown of Osijek after the Balkan Wars. She walks from the station, recalling places that were wiped out by artillery, and with each step the city of her childhood is slowly erased by the vision of a new city, carrying the bitter realization that nothing is in its place and nothing will ever be in its place again. I haven't read the full novel, as it hasn't been translated yet, but I read parts of it as I walked with the guide in the contemporary city. Similarly, in fragments, I watched my own city, Kharkiv, being bombed live by Russian aircraft and shelled by Russian artillery. I watched short videos and newsreels, and, as they piled up, the city that I had left only one month before the full-scale invasion became history.

I remember leaving Kharkiv on a cold January day in 2022, hungover from a party and art exhibition from the night before. When the plane took off from Kharkiv airport for a layover in Istanbul, tears ran down my cheeks, and I couldn't explain this unexpected, bizarre slurry of emotions and mostly slept through the second leg of the flight.[12]

I was a thousand miles away when the full-scale invasion began. I knew the facts. I saw the videos. I knew which among my favorite places had ceased to exist, what parts of the city were being levelled, from day to day. But as long as I was far away, my city

---

11   "A Visit to the Other City", *Months to Years* (Winter 2024), https://monthstoyears.org/a-visit-to-the-other-city/
12   Memory is a funny thing. In an earlier essay, 'Kharkiv is My Home', I am not crying on the plane. Here tears are running down my face. I read it and remember clearly, sitting alone at the front of the plane, whimpering to my own surprise. Then, return to the earlier text, and clearly remember being composed and quietly suffering nausea while watching a cat stroking their cat through the grate of its cage. Both memories live inside of me, and both are as self-assured, as two elderly ladies having their morning espresso at a piazza and gossiping about their neighbours who passed away. So here it is, a glitch in my brain that has no explanation whatsoever. Is it war or is it me? And can we really exist separately at this point?

was still intact, and the news remained a big *Truman Show*-style illusion.

For the first time in my life, I didn't want to go back home. The destiny of Ivana Šojat haunted me. To see it with my own eyes would make it real. To go back would mean to ruin the city that I knew forever. I didn't want the war to be real. Didn't want to see the destroyed Palace of Labour, a grand 1916 Art Nouveau construction that used to connect two historical streets by an arched courtyard.[13] In my mind that building was still there, enveloped by a busy humdrum of passersby and trams, with its herbal apothecary, sneaker-repair shop and café, and murky NGO offices. At one insane moment, a year before, I was thinking of buying one of the tiny condos converted from the former communal flats on the upper floor of the Palace. I did not want to see those last floors gone, the broken windows and the smell of the graveyard cold that comes out of the abandoned houses. Six months before the full-scale invasion, I stood on the observation deck of the twelfth floor of an iconic modernist skyscraper, Derzhprom, and looked at my city of 1.6 million residents below, thinking that it could only get better from here.

The pulsating ache of not knowing got the best of me though. On June 1, 2022 my international passport was stamped, and the train slowly rolled across the Hungarian border. "Is it Ukraine, Mom?" The girl on the seat in front asked, and when the mom said yes, I noticed Ukrainian number plates on the cars waiting at the railway crossing. Strangely, the earth did not explode, the sky didn't turn black, and no sirens could be heard. War is not a cinematic apocalypse; it creeps into you slowly. The air outside was as summery and hot as in Budapest, and the only sign of home was that the train stopped short before the actual platform, and people spilled out across the dusty rails and onto the familiar streets of Mukachevo. A friend from Kharkiv who came to the platform missed me and when we finally met on a scalding dusty street, she

---

13 The construction was started in 1914 and finished in 1916, https://ui.org.ua/en/postcard/palace-of-labour/

asked if I wanted "local food" or "normal food". The Kharkiv snobbery resurfaced, and we went to "the only place they serve decent coffee". It felt like home—we walked and commented on the plurality of secondhand stores selling European stock of last year's collections, musing on how one could live in a place with no metro and no sushi and no boutique wine cafés. But most importantly, I heard about Kharkiv firsthand. My friend's face changed when she learned I was going to Kharkiv. It was clear she did not feel she could ever go back. There was horror and envy in her eyes.

I explained that going back had become my idée fixe precisely because I couldn't live in the suspended state, in which Kharkiv, like Schrödinger's cat, was both alive and dead. During the first week of the big war, I called my dad hysterically (a huge setback after a lifetime spent establishing a limit of two calls per week), and demanded reports on what had blown up where, and how many of our relatives had been shelled or trapped in the occupied territories. I started to care about everyone, including the lady my mom had befriended once long ago when she'd come to sell us milk. Our small, comfortable world—of weekend drives to the countryside, fishing in the Donets River and visiting a horde of distant family I hardly remembered, became as fragile as a porcelain tea set, run over by a Russian tank.

The images of the bombs dropped on Kharkiv's historic center rolled on repeat on major channels across the world, but I skipped them when they appeared. I watched the airstrike on the regional governmental building once, after which my hands started to tremble. In those first, most horrible weeks, ideas popped up in my mind. To go back immediately. Drop the PhD that I'd started at St. Andrews. Cross the border. Reverse the endless tide of refugees fleeing the Ukrainian East. Go to witness and live through the last days of my city, and go down with it, as, if we believe Homer, the Trojans had done. At the same time, I didn't feel like dying. In fact, never had I wanted to survive so very much. Perhaps because, after the initial fears, it soon became clear that the Kharkiv region would stand. I especially wanted to live so that I could see the last Russian leave its borders.

Everything about the invasion was Orwellian. The Russians were orcs, and, funnily, they called us "elves" to show the effeminate nature of our society, weak in their eyes because we did not have a cult of a half-naked sixty-year-old dictator on horseback like they did, in a very manly "orc" kind of style.

The city greeted me with temperatures in the nineties, boiling sun-dried streets, and hot winds that came from the steppe. From the station, I was supposed to go straight to underground and take a metro. It was bizarre that dad didn't meet me as usual on the platform. It was too dangerous, as train stations were targeted by Russian missiles. I touched the cold metal of the metro door handle and stopped. I turned around, and walked out. Walking through the city was the way I appropriated it, made it my own. The taxi drivers shouted out the names of the streets that they were brave enough to take you to. I walked past them and dipped into an old nineteenth-century market neighborhood. A car stopped, and the military asked if I needed help getting anywhere. I shrugged, "No". The suitcase only looked big, but wasn't heavy. Definitely lighter than my nerves.

The first thing you notice in a Ukrainian city close to the frontline is the taped windows. In the early days, locals grabbed any Scotch tape they could get their hands on. Its patterns and multicolored strips could be seen all around, as if we were having a new festival. The tape didn't prevent the window from shattering, but helped to keep the shards of glass from spilling on the people inside.

Kharkiv was quiet, taped. In some places I saw traces of shell damage. In others, traces of gunfire. Not everything was on the news.

Quiet and demure, with distant artillery work, Kharkiv stopped being the city I once knew, my default city. But walking down its streets, alone, except for the occasional person who tried to offer me help—everyone offered help in those days—I also felt relief. For months, the city had been chasing me in dreams, and memories and reveries; and finally, as I walked through its damaged hurting body, it stopped being a painful David Lynch kind of space, the red room in my nightmares. It was still Kharkiv. I took the metro to the station where dad was waiting for me. The house smelled the same, of tomatoes and the soap that mom loved to buy in bulk.

On a jog the next morning, I saw the shell wounds of our house, and stroke it like you would stroke a cat. The ground floor balcony was gone and our neighbor was injured in one of the attacks. Everyone I met as I walked along in my pink jogging pants said hello. Neighbors talked to one another and discussed the particulars of heavy weapon shipping to the country. Shop assistants talked about S-300 missiles and that it was a bad year for cucumbers. Suddenly, the entire city became gentler to one another, holding the doors, saying sorry, trying their best to smile at strangers.

Suddenly the city was more alive than I ever remembered it being. My friends laughed more loudly, and went to all the cultural events, and every reopening of a café, and even the literary snobs who used to never remember my name hugged me on the streets. And I hugged the damaged Palace of Labour, and stroked its fractured walls. It wasn't that bad, I suddenly realized. Kharkiv became a street cat that got out of a fight with a pack of dogs. Its ears were torn in each and every place, and its gaze got weird and rough, but it got out alive. Elves and hobbits walked the streets. And I got a strange tingling wish to smoke a pipe when I saw them and smiled at them.

I cried through the quiet night on a sleeper train taking me away back to the West. Tears, involuntarily, again rolled down a freshly washed train pillowcase, and got into my ears and headphones, making strange messy puddles in my braids. In the next-door compartment, women from Mariupol exchanged news about the occupying army, which had raided their flats. I cried like a thief, quietly, guilty at the happiness that my city was still "ours", that every enemy soldier who tried to enter it was dead and silent, and would never be able to tell friends and family that they "took the city".[14] I tried not to sob too loudly.

---

14   In 2024 I learnt from an interview of a Kharkiv national guardsman on Hromadske media that two of the paratroopers from Pskov were captured alive and later exchanged, and that a medal was created in honor of their brave destruction of our municipal property. I find it perfectly fascinating. A medal for

---

burning a geography classroom, while my unruly classmates were crucified for wearing dirty shoes in ours.

What to Do with All the Russian Books[15]

It's a sweltering summer day in the early 2000s. The Donets River outside the city of Kharkiv in the utmost East of Ukraine. Meadows of tall fluorescent grass and wild chamomiles descend to the water, and sleek black adders run like ribbons under my feet, from one patch of tall grass to the other, making me scream even though the tiny yellow spots on the head hint they aren't really adders. The Donets River carries many myths, shared and my own. There's an old legend of a Cossack mountain above White Lake. There is always a Cossack mountain or a Cossack grave wherever you go in Ukraine. Cossacks, the Ukrainian military class, would often give their fortunes to the monasteries, and spend the rest of their days in these remote refuges of the Field when it was still wild. The Saint Nicholas Monastery, legend has it, was raided by the Russian troops that at the time were ordered to dismantle the Cossack state — the Zaporizhian Sich. The monks, former warriors, put up a fight to defend their property. Realizing they were outnumbered, they jumped off the high hill above the lake. The spirits of the old monks are said to be inhabiting the surrounding forests to this day, and, looking at the fierce resistance that the people of the Kharkiv region displayed in 2022, perhaps, there might be a grain of truth in the old myth.

    I swim, fighting the fast deep river waters, and then, exhausted, climb out onto the tall bank and fall on the hot sand. I cover my face with grandpa's straw hat and daydream about other, newer legends. I think of the dark midsummer night swim when a body got washed up on this beach, rolled into a carpet. The extraordinary event caused an uproar among the locals, who became suddenly wary of the dangerous torrents. A notorious local business queen, Halyna, the owner of the Kharkiv train station's first private saloon, "At Halyna's", became absolutely furious at the idea that

---

15 "What to Do with All the Russian Books", *Fiery Scribe Review* (October 19, 2023), https://www.fieryscribereview.com.ng/2023/10/what-to-do-with-all-russian-books.html

her perfect beach was ruined, so she hired a priest to consecrate the sands and the changing cabins with the holy water. World balance was restored.

The most recent myth was a small-scale alien invasion in itself. Locals called it "the summer of the Sea Cabbage Plague". The story has it, an unfortunate stranger threw the contents of an aquarium with an exotic predatory plant, *Pistia*, into the river. *Pistia* started to breed so fast it hindered water flow, threatening ecological disaster. I remember a rowing weekend down the river, when our entire boat fought through the thick layer of this "sea cabbage". We threw it on the banks, away, and sometimes at one another, pretending it was about to stick into our faces like a horror movie beast. Ecologists were pessimistic, saying the new species would kill fish and dry side streams (killing every life form, of course). Then winter came, and the tropical cabbage froze, vanishing like the aliens in H. G. Wells's *War of the Worlds*.

The Donets River remembers many legends and writers. And writers remember the Donets too. Written in 1932, Maik Yohansen's *Dr. Leonardo's Journey to Sloboda Switzerland* almost perfectly aligns with the area of my childhood summer holidays. This frivolously humorous text could be a delightful read on Halyna's holy beach. But growing up I never knew about Dr. Leonardo or Maik Johansen. The book was banned by the Soviet Ministry of Culture, and the memory of Dr. Leonardo forgotten. Its author Maik Johansen was executed by the Soviet secret police, and rumor has it that the legendary fourth part of *Dr. Leonardo* is still hidden in one of the Moscow dungeons.

There are other, very famous texts that tell about the Donets River. The medieval *Tale of Bygone Years* mentions it as a wild nomadic stream that brought predators to the kingdom of Kyivan Rus, a predatory state in itself. *The Tale of Igor's Campaign* tells about the Kyivan Prince Ihor, who decided once to attack Polovtsians (for whatever reason, god only knows), and got captured in the fields of the Donets instead. The *Tale* was written by a Kyivan monk, Nestor, about Kyiv's prince, but for some reason we were never allowed to think of him as "ours", as the heritage of Kyiv was taken by Moscow. The old tales were too valuable to be considered

Ukrainian, and so we were not allowed to think of them as local, and even in my school years we studied these texts in the Foreign Literature course.

The silencing and physical destruction of one part of Ukrainian literature, and denying us the right for the other part, has been the reason why I never read about the Donets during my summer holidays on its banks. Our lake houses were filled with books, but few of them spoke to us or about us. The stacks of Soviet volumes people brought to the countryside rot and burn did not count. Those were books about a soviet man (mostly men). The perfect heroic stories of pioneer kids and the communist party, unbearably naive, blah and sterile.

Growing up 30 kilometers from the Russian border was in a sense like living in the vicinity of the Chernobyl power plant, where instead of radiation, the remainder of sovietness leaked out. During the first years of Ukrainian independence, this decomposing sovietness was still visible and palpable in every pore of our young Ukrainian state. Of course, for me, Ukraine was something eternal, its silhouette fixated on my school map and my eyelids, 603,000 km^2. The Soviet past was recent, but imaginary, an anecdote that could well be a plot of my grandpa's vivid imagination. Kharkiv was just a storage of things left from this fictional past—an "antresoli" (Russian word for upped storage closet space under the ceiling) for a huge number of Soviet books, things, and myths.

I never understood how those books got in, but they were in every house and flat that I saw. Mom explained that oftentimes Soviet people had to buy those books, as an extra condition if they wanted to purchase something more practical. A winter jacket, leather boots, or toilet paper.

At my friend's lake house, by the fast steppe Donets River, I saw three identical volumes of *How the Steel Was Tempered* by a Russian writer Ostrovsky. All three books were glued together, never touched by a human hand. They were lying there, at a summer house, from the dawn of time, like theatre props. My friend's dad would read a two-year-old gossip newspaper lying on a deck chair in between potato weeding sessions. But never Ostrovsky, God forbid.

Several years ago, I watched "The Danger of a Single Story", a brilliant talk on how it feels to be surrounded by an imperial culture that does not speak about you. Chimamanda Ngozi Adichie recalls how she'd always dreamt of apples instead of oranges and saw herself as a white boy instead of a curly Black girl, because that was what British novels for little white British boys were about. Soviet and Russian imperial books worked in a similar way. I could never recognize myself and my home on their pages. Kharkiv never seemed to be a hero of the Soviet russophone books that surrounded me, making me think that it was too small, too insignificant, less photogenic than "a provincial town N", which Russian writers seemed to be obsessed with. In my imagination Russia consisted of three cities, Moscow, Petersburg, and a "provincial town N". Ukrainian literature seemed to consist of villages, where everyone was a slave or a poor woman made to sell her virtue to the Russians.

Sometimes I could recognize Kharkiv in the foreign writers like Mykola Gogol (as I thought of him then). We were not allowed to think of him as Ukrainian, because people said it was only "Russian literature that walked out of Gogol's overcoat", and because Gogol was "a good writer".

Yet, every other Saturday morning, Mom would take me on the metro to Kharkiv city center. As we walked from the History Museum down the Bursatskyi Descent, one of the oldest city roads, leading from the original fortress down to the riverside market, I always remembered Gogol's novella, called Vij. The text starts with a merry bunch of students running out of the *bursa* (religious college) down to the market, grabbing every kind of food on their way without payment as they head out home for their spring break. While Gogol didn't write about Kharkiv per se, he described a typical Ukrainian town, and his description fits Kharkiv like a glove.

Like Gogol's characters, we walked down the Descent leading from the former *bursa* school down to the market. There, in a labyrinth of market rows surrounded by bucolic eighteenth-century two-story buildings, books, notepads and all kinds of stationery would be sold, cheap paperbacks and even cheaper smuggled reprints of Oxbridge language manuals. Up a narrow Classical alley, ambiguously Soviet-dressed people were selling the exact books that I never read. Unbeknownst to me their lives were filled with adventure, trickstering old ladies out of precious collections, and other drama. I learned about it from the book one of them wrote and congenially sold me many years later, as an addition to the 1960s Kharkiv photo album, which I needed as desperately as a Soviet person needed a Yugoslavian winter jacket.

As I grew up, Ukrainian books started to become more popular, and the old book market was replaced by pretty bookshops where book assistants smiled at you and spoke in Ukrainian. Smiling and the Ukrainian language became the new signs of Kharkiv intellectuals. In the late 1990s, Kharkiv became the center of the Ukrainian printing industry, and we were lucky to have those first editions of recovered and rediscovered Ukrainian classics, and new unbearably postmodernist authors. In the secondhand Classical descent part, though, Ukrainian books were rare guests. Just like in home libraries. To get a two-volume set of Olha Kobylyanska, the main feminist Ukrainian writer of the early 1900s, was as difficult as getting to the North Pole expedition. Every Ukrainian book printed before Ukrainian independence was a miracle, a survivor of censorship and a proof that someone in those years spent their entire lives fighting for this book to see the light of day.

The first Ukrainian literature textbooks were a trial-and-error, and only now that I've started to teach Ukrainian to beginners, I realize how hard it must have been to take those first steps. Unlike Russian, Ukrainian literature consisted mostly of banned authors. These authors were not merely sent away to Caucasus, like Alexander Pushkin, but rather shot, like reindeer (like Maik Johansen), subjected to psychiatric treatment (like Volodymyr Sosiura), broken psychologically (like Pavlo Tychyna), driven to suicide (like Mykola Khvylyovy) or, like Ostap Vyshnia, sent to build the Trans-Siberian express so adored by romantic foreign tourists.

My mom never believed that writers like Maik Johansen or Vasyl Stus existed, because she had never heard of them in her Soviet school. She consequently did not believe they were important, and didn't help me read them. This added to my perception of these writers' biographies. I did not believe that Maik Yohansen could be arrested in Kharkiv, in plain sight, just several miles from my home, and simply killed, in the same year when a Russian writer Maxim Gorky was sunbathing on Capri. Was he better than Yohansen if everyone in the Soviet schools read him? I was not sure.

In contrast to Russian literature, quite abstract and philosophical, showing very little detail of the actual life of everyday humans, Ukrainian literature was overwhelmed with the tiniest details, and smallest social injustices towards just about every creature, from a lumberjack's son to a forest nymph. It seemed that there were absolutely no historical times when Ukrainian writers and people did not suffer. We always complained. Shevchenko complained about Russians, Poles, Turks, Jews, Ukrainians who were rich and enslaved other Ukrainians. The only ones who Shevchenko cared for were cherry trees, poor peasant women who had to harvest grain all the time between the times they fell victims of Russian soldiers (oh how differently does it sound now in 2023). Panas Myrnyi complained about Russians and the enslavement of Ukrainian farmers. Panteleimon Kulish complained about Russians, Turks, Poles and Ukrainians bickering between themselves only to be enslaved by Russians, Turks, Poles, and so on. Olha Kobylanska complained about toxic men and poor women who could not earn their living honestly (she lived in Austro-Hungarian empire, and didn't get to complain about Russians. Lesya Ukrainka complained about Russians and the impossibility of forest nymphs to live amongst the greedy Ukrainian villagers. Ivan Bahrany complained about Russians and Soviet concentration camps. Oksana Zabuzhko complained about Russians, Americans and weak-willed Ukrainian intellectuals who could not imagine the independent Ukrainian identity. Yuri Andrukhovych complained about women in general, and Russians of course.

In short, most Ukrainian writers in our school curriculum complained about Russians. While Russians themselves—I saw it clearly in the course of Foreign Literature—did not think about Ukrainians a single bit, enjoying their fabulous bohemian melancholies and ball dancing. Only later did I realize that aggressors usually prefer to be silent about their victims.

Speaking about her recent book *Russia's War*, Jade McGlynn mentions that Russia's neighbors often see Russian culture as a vampire culture. This definition might seem slightly *Twilight*-like at first. But it sinks in. Vampires have three strategies towards their victims, to kill, to make subservient, or to convert.

In his novel *The White Guard*, a Russian writer Mikhail Bukgakov shows Kyiv, a city of his birth, through the eyes of a small-time Russian gentry who watch with horror as Ukrainian elites rapidly flip Kyiv into a Ukranian city the moment the Russian empire collapses. In a way, the Russian state sees Ukrainians and other colonized peoples as shapeshifters who put up with imperial rules, emulate behaviors of Russians, even learn to speak without an accent, but only up to a certain point. Russia always fears that they would convert back in a blink of an eye, and reveal the savage identity of the Other the moment imperial ties are relaxed. Thus, Ukrainians can never be trusted. Bulgakov accurately conveys this primordial Russian fear of Ukrainians, the aliens in the crowd.

Bulgakov's Kyiv is small and suffocating. It is nothing like the bucolic, sunny, ornamental and boundless city of Ivan Nechuy-Levytsky, or the ambitious megapolis of Lina Kostenko. In short, it is not the center of the world, like it is for any Ukrainian writer. And rightly so. *The White Guard* is not about the entire Kyiv, but rather a small fracture of it, the world of the Russian minority. A desolate, crumbling world of people who suddenly felt that everyone around them threw their human Russian skins off to become something else, Ukrainians. A Ukrainian leader Petlura, whose surname the characters of *The White Guard* are afraid to pronounce, studied at the same university as Bulgakov, almost at the same time. How can an educated polyglot suddenly turn against the empire, and call the peasants to revolt?

The Maidan revolution of 2014 was shown by the Russian state TV much like Bulgakov showed Petlura. The great Russian writer and a tiny Russian TV propagandist see Ukrainians in the same way. As dangerous shapeshifters.

Perhaps, I think, the college educated Petlura, the founder of the first Ukrainian embassies, a man who died in Paris in exile, who was not a thinker of an imperial scale, but was a visionary. It is just that Bulgakov could not see Kyiv in the way Petlura and other Ukrainians did. And yet, when you ask any Russian doing literary studies abroad, if they know the greatest novel about Kyiv, they would most probably say, "*The White Guard*".

If you ask a Ukrainian, they would nominate a different book, *The City* (*Misto*) by Valerian Pidmohylnyi. The events of *The City* take place several years after The White Guard. A young man from a village arrives in the big city to become a great writer. The city opens up slowly, revealing first its faraway fringes with the islands of Dnipro River, spanning to the multi-story houses with elevators, where the young writer's love affairs take place. Perhaps, he also walks up the Andriyivskyy Descent, and looks at the house of Bulgakov, thinking that he could have never been allowed inside just several years back. The cynical life of the city slowly wears down the writer's enthusiasm. He grows bored and disillusioned with fame. Kyiv is shown as a boundless universe with its hidden treasures and dark histories, and moral corruption. For a Ukrainian writer Kyiv is the center of the world, while for Bulgakov it is a small provincial town. Not because Kyiv is small, but because Russian Kyiv is small, like every diaspora's neighbourhood.

Slowly, as Ukraine re-evaluates its colonial history, more and more books about our cities resurface, and yet more are being written. These literary works mark a wall rising between the two states, as we start to recognize ourselves on printed pages of books that not many Russians will ever open. This wall grows in many, often anecdotal fields as well. In a recent book of reportages about the town of Severodonetsk, now temporarily occupied, Svitlana Oslavska recounts that, in 2014, the Donbas criminal world chose the Ukrainian side for a very simple reason, "in Ukraine, the most North we could be sent to is Chernihiv, a mild continental climate, while if we join Russia, we could go to Siberia. And so, we prefer Donbas to stay in Ukraine".

This very practical reason is also why I today reread all those Ukrainian novels that I could not find at school. On my shelf new *Tiger Trappers* by Ivan Bahranyi stand alongside Maik Yohansen and his *Dr. Leonardo's Journey to Sloboda Switzerland with His Future Lover, the Beautiful Alcesta*. Both books are new editions, in a trendy design, with the commentary of a well-known Ukrainian literary critic. Both books aren't written by the great Russian writers, and thank God for that, I think. I enjoy reading these novels partly because they are thrilling and fresh, partly because they speak about my world, about Donets, Kharkiv and Poltava, as the places worthy of attention. These are also the texts and places and rivers Ukrainians continue to die for as I write these texts. Perhaps Russian soldiers also think of these places as worthy to die for. Not many highbrow Western professors write articles about these books, much less than they write about abstract Dostoyevsky sufferings. But I think they should reconsider. To my mind, Ukrainian literature and language hold some important keys to the nature of this war, and the resistance of Ukrainians, the Frodo Baggins of contemporary Europe, the kids-who-survived, whichever franchise you prefer. Just like great Russian novels hold some important clues to why their great Russian people cannot stop loving "thy neighbors" to death.

What to do with all those Russian books in our lake house libraries? I don't know the answer to that question yet. On a hot summer day, I take a bunch of them to a newly opened Media Café in central Kharkiv. The books are taken to recycling, money used to support a local military division that didn't let Kharkiv be occupied. Perhaps, we will have to use other Russian books to make fires, if more attacks on the energy infrastructure takes place in the upcoming winter. What I know is that my library is slowly growing with Ukrainian books, and I finally begin to recognize myself and the great wild river of the Donets on their pages.

Merla,
The River and the Goddess[16]

On a map, the Kharkiv region is shaped like a heart. In reality—or, rather, in my head—it has always looked like the two halves of an apple. One half started along the former Moscow Avenue, now Heroes of Kharkiv Avenue, in the kernel of the city. It ran out and past the mountains of Izyum and deep into the wild fields of Donbas. This was my half. In the early twentieth century, my great grandpa traveled from here abroad to earn hard coin working in the fields of rich farmers. There, he met my great grandma, who came with the same purpose from the same village. They returned together and never parted. With him, great grandma drilled for the exams at Kharkiv University, with him she managed a House of Culture in a newly founded little town in Donbas. When, in 1937, he was sentenced to death by Stalin for being Ukrainian in 1937, she took his kids and fled back, and lived in that half, along the wild and cruel river of Donets River that flows into the somber Russian river Don, witness of great tragedies and the genocides of many indigenous peoples of the Caucasus. In 2022, the forests, rivers and villages of my ancestors were occupied. The occupation lasted for six months, but this brief period changed the land. As I came over to our formerly occupied lake house in the summer of 2023, I realized that my walking space shrunk to a quarter of a hectare of our family garden. Nothing else was safe. The field where I used to mindlessly gather wildflowers, fearing only snakes, was spattered with warnings: "Mines". The forest was closed with barbed wire. The lake beach was empty in the height of summer. "Mines" signs were everywhere. There is a phrase in Russian fairy tales: "It smells of Russian spirit". When the old witch, Baba Yaga, comes into her house, she knows if there is an intruder; she cries out, "It smells of Russian spirit!". Driving through my part of the Kharkiv region, along the wild Donets River, I smelled Russian spirit: burnt cars by the side of the road, blown-apart bridges, shelled village huts. Thoughts

---
16 "Merla: The River and the Goddess", *Crab Creek Review* (Spring 2024).

kept revolving in my mind. *I don't like this place anymore. It doesn't feel like my home. It doesn't feel safe.* My river and my meadow sprinkled with mines for decades... Will my future kids ever walk my great-grandpa's forest paths?

I started to think about the other half of the Kharkiv region, which snakes through the green hills in the direction of Kyiv. This side of Kharkiv's apple/heart beats along the Merla River. In old Slavic lore, Merla was the goddess of death. When Ukrainian settlers came here in the seventeenth century, they were surprised by the slow, "dead" waters of the local serpentine rivers. At an unhurried pace, Merla flows into the Vorskla, the home river of Gogol and many other gothic Ukrainian writers. The Vorskla then flows into the Dnipro, the soulmate of all Ukrainians; the sacred waters of "Father Dnipro" are said to protect "Mother Ukraine". Kharkiv drinks from Dnipro with one half and from the Don, the tragic, harsh river where Ukrainians came to be cleansed, "Russified", and ultimately wiped out, with the other. The part of the region where Merla flows wasn't occupied. A small bus running every two hours from the Kharkiv Central Market drops me off at the village's central square in Merchyk, a mere intersection of two roads with several shops, a post office, and a Soviet statue of an unknown soldier from World War II. My friend, who lives here says people have come from Kharkiv and de-occupied parts recently. The unexpected influx of semi-displaced or sort-of-displaced folks — to be officially considered displaced persons, they must leave their region — brought businesses and activities, pizza delivery, manicures, and yoga.

The Soviet statue distracts attention from the park and a ruined mansion hiding in the formerly exotic botanical garden of the Shydlovsky dynasty. Further down the crooked road, more imported gardens and mansions pop up. Most belonged to nineteenth-century sugar industrialists. Nearby one of the Parkhomivka sugar estates, the young Kazimir Malevich, the avant-garde artist, lived for a time, as his father was the manager of the sugar factory. Malevich learned to make paints by looking at how villagers did it when decorating their house walls. Perhaps, the artist's first work could be found somewhere on a ruined hut we pass by. Estates, ponds, and gardens with exotic flowers were rewilded, giving way to new forest species, part of the Merla's witchy charm. The river is always slightly hidden; you need to rub it from the dirt to find a treasure. Merla's land is interesting this way, reminding me of the city of Kharkiv itself, which does not boast its treasures. Neither does Merla. The goddess of death and the slow eastern Ukrainian rivers get under my skin, and I start to ask questions. I wonder about the local language. My friend says it is very much Surzhyk, a mixture of Ukrainian and Russian, but to my ear, used to the other side, it sounds almost perfectly Ukrainian. With long oooo's and the swallowing of some endings, the local phonetics is soft and bewitching. The people of the Merla have a slightly different melody, relaxed if compared to my native somber and militant Donets half.

We swim in the pond and talk about the local *verguny* enterprise. *Verguny*, traditional Ukrainian pastries that look like donuts, are becoming more popular with city-dwellers who dig into their roots, trying to understand what makes them Ukrainians, the endangered species. Traditions hold longer here on this side of Kharkiv region, hampered by the slow waters and peaceful fields. Two sleepy policemen drive past us indifferently on a sunflower road; we pick at a young, juicy sunflower we'd torn off just out of curiosity.

It is only when the deafening air raid shakes the Merchyk that I wake up to realize, it is just the second half of the same apple. When one half starts to rot, it is only so long until the other half begins. Or maybe it isn't an apple after all, but the right half of the Kharkiv heart-apple? The traditional blue colors of local emblems and house decorations, like venous blood, cool and calm down the tumultuous arterial left side, pulsating red as Russian troops fight and drown in the Donets River. The two sides of the Kharkiv region, like the two halves of the heart, make the organism work. People fleeing from the dread and mass graves of Izyum find temporary refuge and peace in the sleepy coolness of Merla. She might well be the goddess of death, but as Donets, her male counterpart, the god of war, boils with blood, Merla sings a lullaby, "Sleep for now, hush, my baby, it will all pass too". The more I look at its lethargic flow, the less I feel like giving up on my broken Donets homeland. Occupied, liberated, traumatized for decades to come, the high proud banks of the Donets are still part of the equation. In time, I will come back to it, and stand on the tall bank looking at Izyum. I will stand on Mount Kremenets amidst the stone Polovets idols, babas, guardians of the ancient nomadic graves. From there, I always feel like I see the entire country: all my fragile, fractured rivers, slow and fast, surviving and healing. Meanwhile Merla, the goddess of death, can bring temporary sleep for those whose heart beats with her.

I started to write "Such a Warm, Such an Early April" on the terrace of a small Black Honey coffee shop in Lviv, in Kryva Lypa Lane – a tiny hipster nook that looked like safety. Powdered sugar from a freshly baked cherry strudel sprinkled the keyboard of my laptop, and fashionable teenagers in oversized everything mixed with traditional Ukrainian embroidery chatted under the crooked linden tree in front. A week later, going back to Kharkiv for Easter, I sat on the equally sunny terrace of the Mr. Bourbon coffee place, eating a cherry pie with more cherries than dough and tasted as I imagined the pie in the famous Twin Peaks diner. Across the road a damaged Slovo House stood, with new residents from Czechia exploring the city. I love to think of writing as an excuse to get a coffee and the biggest dessert available.

Such a Warm, Such an Early April

In 1981 a star of the Ukrainian poetic cinema, Ivan Mykolaychuk, directed *Such a Late, Such a Warm Autumn*. The film tells the story of a Ukrainian migrant visiting his home towards the end of Soviet times, and is, in truth, a requiem to the impossibility of returning to places that have changed forever. The Soviet border appeared eternal, impregnable, like a two-sided prison, separating families, dividing human bodies from their minds, lingering in the lands of memory as though in purgatory. A generational trauma of the hero or my parents' generation was that leaving always came with a hopeless "forever".

The same rigid border concealed Ukraine from the rest of the world throughout the twentieth century. Not many knew about Kharkiv, the second largest city of Ukraine, itself the largest country in Europe, owing to the shadow the Soviet border cast on all the colonized peoples. Beyond a simple physical line, the border obscured knowledge production and prevented local cultures from speaking for and about themselves. English translations of classic Ukrainian authors such as Lesia Ukrainka or Olha Kobylyanska are still rare in bookshops and otherwise vast British libraries, dominated by imperial Russian titles. A list of Kharkiv authors killed by Stalin's repression stretches on the walls of the Slovo House on the central Kulture Street, along with traces of recent aerial bombardment by the contemporary Russian state.

As the Russian military command makes its third attempt in the past hundred years to erase the city, I sit at a café overlooking the house of executed Ukrainian writers, sip filtered coffee, produced in the former British colonies, and think about the meaning of free will. More importantly, I ask myself, why are the city's 1.3 million residents so obstinate in their attempts to stay in this unnaturally warm, violent spring of 2024, in this tortured land?

--

April walks into Kharkiv like fever enters a body, with discomfort. The sudden blasts of wind bring sands from the Sahara desert on top of the usual dust and dandelions of the Wild Field. Hot air follows the Saharan sands, making all the fruit trees blossom at once–apricots, cherries, plums and apples, even the pears look out shyly. This year is an anomaly. Like the previous year was an anomaly, and the year before. We have been living through ten years of anomalies, rains of twisted metal shreds and bombs falling on our heads from the planes our forebears built for the great Soviet empire. The empire punishes us, the descendants of nuclear physicists and tank manufacturers, for breaking free.

Kharkiv's historical center sits in the valley formed by three slow steppe rivers, Kharkiv, Lopan and Udy. Thin snake-like waters of the rivers nurture the soil of the city, and wild orchards devour any architecture, as if trying to hide fragile buildings from the new guided bombs. Who are the inventors concocting new kinds of bombs to fall on us, I wonder, walking along the riverside. Do they live in private houses, or apartment buildings, do their window panes tremble at night? Do they eat oatmeal or eggs for breakfast?

Bombs fall at random, on hot weekend afternoons, to drive the local citizens to flee, clearing space for Russian officers, their wives and their children, who would play with Chinese toy cars we bought for our kids, nephews and nieces. The breath of the Russian officers grows closer. But, for some reason, Kharkivians aren't in a hurry to run. They wash their windows before Holy Week, bake Easter breads and paint their fragile walls in superior violet shades, mixed for them at builders' supermarkets. The green urban jungle, the gardens, courtyards and country house orchards are carefully weeded. Bright tulips are planted around monuments previously covered with sandbags and safety nets. Saharan winds tear at the nets, and the eyes of Kharkiv poets, our angry geniuses, look out. The elbow belonging to one of the lovers on Architect Square becomes exposed and freezes on a cold April night.

"Aunt Zyna paid for three months' electricity at the lake house. I want to pay for a year, but maybe three months is smart", dad says, as he pours corn kernels into warm water in preparation for his Saturday drive to the garden. "We might have the time to harvest the first crops, it will take time for them to occupy us again," he concludes, calculating how many monthly payments would be required for the Russian troops to occupy our lake house again as they did in early 2022. Planting corn is a sign of optimism, belief that in August we would be able to harvest. Bombs glide into the park, falling near the monument of Soviet repression. Wiry Kharkiv pensioners jog past the crater down the oldest bicycle lane, passing a white cyclist monument. Nature is persistent. It is natural to enjoy April in the Wild Field. All its heart-stopping abundance of life forms blossom in white and pink across the city, making people suffering from allergies take flight or turn to heavy drugs. Nature becomes wild and beautiful like an ancient nomadic goddess, and heavy storms are tinged by the sky so electrically blue that you have to ask if it isn't virtual reality already.

Springs in the Ukrainian east are painfully beautiful. Like the Northern Lights, they take your breath away, in a matter of days changing the fragile land, snowy valleys becoming an endless fluorescent green. Every spring that we survive adds to the the local population's resilience and immortality. Kharkiv is a city guarded by World War II mobile mechanical guns, which drive and — quite surprisingly — manage to deal with kamikaze drones owing to the brilliance of the air defense operators. The operators know the price, as they guard their own houses, their kids asleep in bathtubs on those turbulent nights of mass attacks. The sirens wail for sixteen hours.

The old machine guns cannot protect a power plant from ballistic missiles, and so the city sinks into darkness and generators' hum. Suddenly, the beauty of the spring becomes sharper, more painful, more unfair. How can this divine landscape exist amidst all of the injustice and us being hunted so viciously? How can we be murdered without any consequences to the killer? Is it because our grandparents created those deadly weapons for the Soviet empire? Kharkiv, the centre of the machine-building industry, the birthplace of the T-34 tank.

Everything seems unreal as I walk to the bus stop as the metro freezes in a blackout. It's summer hot. Walking in a T-shirt, I fight white apricot petals that tingle my skin as they waltz persistently and land and mix in my hair. The sunlight is so naked and pure and brutal that a single solar battery, it feels, could power the whole of Kharkiv.

Green city buses, flashing electric letters, "Universitetska", pull up at the entrance to the metro. Today the metro would function as a bomb or nuclear disaster shelter — depending on the will of our neighbors.

So why the hell are we staying put? Is it because May in the Wild Field is even prettier than April? Walking the cobblestoned hill up from the river, to the ghost of the old Kharkiv fortress, breathing heavily, I think that the worst is yet to come.

"It's not that bad," thousands of locals mumble into inquisitive mobile phones. "Thank you, we will take it into consideration that you have a half house free on the Right Bank". The right Bank of the Dnipro, the safe bank, the boring bank of the Dnipro.

One night after a meteor falls somewhere in the outskirts, lilacs occupies every patch of breathing air, every corner of every red brick mansion of the old downtown. Like the Germans in World War II, lilac occupies Kharkiv twice. First, in violet; then, towards May, the white flowers come. White lilac is so fearless it grows on the balconies of old paper mills.

On my birthday, a total blackout happens. We walk to the Lopan River, the old cathedral looks like the Cheshire cat, its stripes so sly and mischievous. The restaurant is dark, trembling in the candlelight. A tremendous silver candelabra on an oval table flickers, and the entire gathered company starts to laugh. We are in a new Middle Ages, the knights and ladies of the round table. On the wall above, a guardian angel made of wire and steel protects the walls from North Korean missiles. Vlad Yudin, a local artist, supplied such a reimagined urban guardian of rusty wires for every spot in town he considered significant.

Everything is more significant in complete darkness. Sounds and smells grip you, taking you from one hearth to another. We drift to a garden bar by the river, and into a different epoch: 1920s cocktails, small tables, the lost generation, talk about how everyone spent the last days in the city before the big war. Prior to the curfew we make one last drift. We dive into another war, the Georgian one, and orange wine brings the air of occupied Abkhazia in Kharkiv's dark downtown. The night air is filled with quiet persistent life. When a taxi driver drops me off by the metro, which on this night has not turned into a nuclear shelter, a young man in the military takes my seat. Twenty minutes before the curfew, everyone wants to be home, as though giant tentacled monsters would be loosed the second the clock strikes 11 p.m.

An old Ukrainian legend has it that at one time a giant three-headed snake settled on the hills near Kyiv. The monster demanded that the Kyivans bring it young girls as a sacrifice. If this demand wasn't fulfilled the three-headed snake would fly through the city, setting fire to its streets and killing any life in its way. When there were no more girls left, except for the princess, the city heads sent a delegation to the strongest man, Mykyta, a leather-maker. Five thousand children whose fathers had been killed by the snake went to beg Mykyta's help. Mykyta's heart melted and he ended up defeating the monster. I recently re-read this story in a version by a poet, Ivan Drach, thinking about sacrifice — Moldova, Georgia, Syria, Chechnya, Ukraine — and what it takes to understand the nature of the three-headed snake.

In the last days of April, the city witnessed red Northern Lights. It was something that had never happened before. Kharkiv locals couldn't enjoy the sight, however. It was long past curfew. Preparations for Orthodox Easter were in full swing. Hot sweet breads were being baked in thousands of kitchens, adding the scent of vanilla, rum and raisins to the street aroma of white lilac.

"Why don't we leave?", I thought, looking at the full moon that licked the sweet sugary cream on top of my freshly baked Easter bread, great-grandma's recipe. Sitting by the tall window of my parents' house I heard the artillery of the invading army, trying to capture the land of my great-grandparents. I sighed, breathing in vanilla, thinking that the worst was yet to come. But also, that the best was yet to come as well.

In the summer of 2023, nukes returned to the menu of potential Ukrainian possibilities. All the national and world news outlets screamed about Russia nuking Ukraine in the days to come. The occupied Zaporizhia Nuclear Power Plant was reported as the likely source of a future attack. An atmosphere of innervation and strange excitement gripped the city. My dad would send photos of himself sitting in an old Soviet gasmask at his office desk. Radio programs invited nuclear physicists and ecologists to explain how a potential radioactive cloud would move over our region. An exact date — July 5 — was given for the purported disaster. After washing my hair with shampoo (but not using conditioner as it could prevent radiation washing off), I would lie on my bed, cover my face with a white sheet — the summer was extremely hot — and count the moments until the end of our world finally began. In those days my PhD supervisor Victoria was very helpful, writing and cheering me up. In one of our exchanges, she suggested that I see Christopher Nolan's newly released Oppenheimer and write a review, from the perspective of someone in Kharkiv. The Conversation, a UK educational media outlet, was also interested. So I had to survive up until the Ukrainian film release on July 20 (one day earlier than in the US, the authors maybe wanting to indulge Ukrainians before our inevitable nuclear demise). I sat next to a bunch of stray teenagers devouring popcorn (both teenagers and I did the devouring), and semi-enjoying the whole thing. When I returned home, before the curfew, the review wrote itself in about two hours. This almost compulsive desire to write quickly is characteristic of most of the essays in this book, but is especially true of this one.

Me: wonderful, nuclear threat survived
My dad on Viber: "preparing for the nuclear explosion".

I Watched Christopher Nolan's *Oppenheimer* in Ukraine
His Greek Tragedy Is Our Reality[17]

Following the recent release of Wes Anderson's *Asteroid City*, Christopher Nolan's *Oppenheimer* continues to infuse the summer of 2023 with atomic energy. Stylistically, of course, the two couldn't be more different. What Anderson shows as a blast outside a diner's windows that doesn't so much as interrupt the characters' coffee, Nolan shapes into a three-hour epic. And as a Ukrainian, I am grateful for that.

While daily life in our wartime state consistently fluctuates between feeling like a farce and a Greek tragedy, Oppenheimer emphasizes the reality of the threat—something, I often feel, that western Europe and the wider world don't fully grasp.

Nolan's Greek tragedy is the world that I live in. Seeing *Oppenheimer* in my local cinema in Kharkiv I hope that—to a smaller degree—a global audience will experience Ukraine's everyday anxiety too.

Nolan's use of sound is what makes his take different from the many other Oppenheimer biopics. So much so that I would see it in the cinema again, purely to focus on how various pieces of music, noises and silences guide the viewer's attention.

As my seat shakes from the stereo effects, nobody in the nearly full cinema flinches. The teenagers to my right are as used to explosions as J. Robert Oppenheimer himself. The moments of silence (a Nolan trademark), however, feel ominous.

It is said that you will never hear "your" missile—the one that kills you. Locals in Kharkiv use this wisdom to calm our nerves after hearing a loud explosion. As we sit through the nearly three-

---

17 "I watched Christopher Nolan's Oppenheimer in Ukraine: his Greek tragedy is our reality", *The Conversation*, July 21, 2023, https://theconversation.com/i-watched-christopher-nolans-oppenheimer-in-ukraine-his-greek-tragedy-is-our-reality-210206

hour film, our only wish is not to hear the bomb siren sound outside, since it would mean we would have to leave the cinema and go to the underground shelter.

Granted that, in a city so close to the border, shelters aren't of much use. It takes about thirty seconds for an S-300 missile to fly from the nearby Russian town of Belgorod, meaning we often hear the siren after the blast. Unsurprisingly, the sound of explosions is a leitmotif in the film, making its soundscape very relatable.

What Nolan gets wrong

The overarching motif of Oppenheimer is a warning against the precarious reality that Ukrainians live in now. As Bohr notes to Oppenheimer, "it's a new world". This warning shapes the symphonic structure of the film, perhaps the most mature of Nolan's works.

Oppenheimer is true to Nolan's greatest cinematic talents. But it speaks to his weaknesses as well. Oppenheimer's children don't get any screen time, but are shown through a nagging baby cry. Women fall similarly short of becoming real, depicted simply as dedicating their lives to Oppenheimer.

I appreciate Nolan not trying to crawl into someone else's skin, instead opting to explore the perspective (that of a white, privileged man) he can personally empathize with. But as a viewer on the other side of nuclear anxiety, I found the film's depth of representation lacking.

Nolan's broad strokes, though powerful, miss detail. The USSR is called "Russia" and Soviet scientists are called "Russians" throughout the film. Seeing it only a few kilometers from the Ukrainian lab that split the first lithium atom in the USSR, this felt ironic.

The massive shelling of the nuclear research reactor by the Russian military in 2022 created an uproar in my local community precisely because so many people here have family and friends who work in physics. Ukraine's nuclear research program, which had been a subject of great pride, was now endangered. In painting all the Soviet scientists in the film as Russians, *Oppenheimer* ignores the work of actual Ukrainian physicists.

In the end, *Oppenheimer* is not a film about historical accuracy or justice, but rather a great emotional and sensory experience. And for a summer blockbuster, what more can one ask?

As I walk out of the cinema, the siren starts to roar, signaling that somewhere in the depths of Russia, a fighter jet carrying ballistic missiles has taken off, harmonious with the last scene of Nolan's film.

I walk through the warm summer evening, feeling strangely more like a Wes Anderson character than a Nolan one. Perhaps, I think, if the explosion blasts behind my back, I won't even drop my mint lemonade. Because I already live in the "new world" of dark nuclear absurdity — one that not even Oppenheimer himself could possibly have predicted.

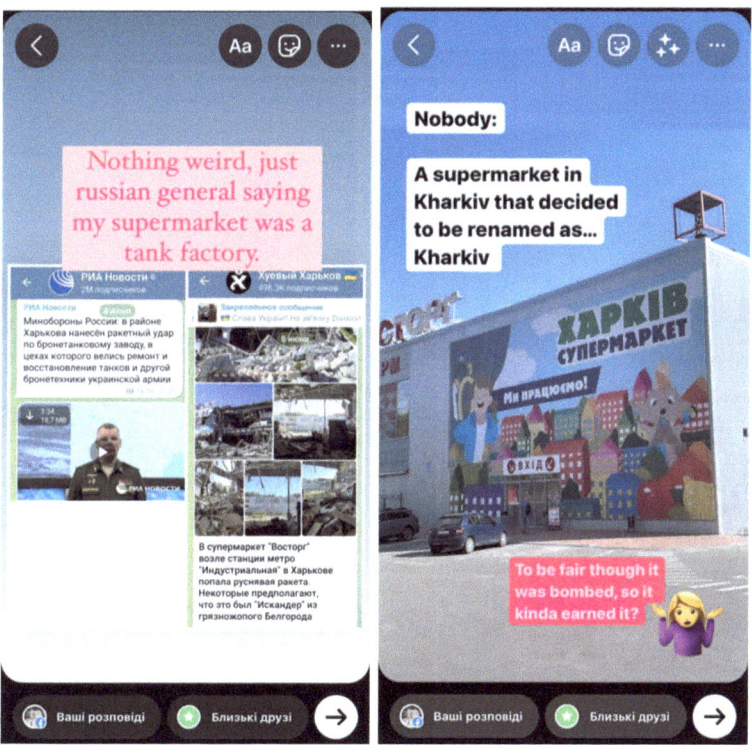

A City Big, But Not Great[18]

"It is a big city, but not a great one," Mykola Khvylovy writes in his deeply insightful, quirky modernist text, *Editor Kark*, laying a sobering hand on Kharkiv's shoulder. In the same text he mentions Hryhorii Skovoroda, a major Ukrainian philosopher who walked the city. "Hryhorii Savvych—as the Russian intelligentsia prefers it", he continues with a smirk, hinting at the all-encompassing attempts of the Russian people to change and twist and reshape non-Russian names, adding patronyms to everything—patronizing our names and cities, adding strange Russian sounds—"a" instead of "o" as in "Adesssa" (for Odesa), and "o" instead of "i" in KharkOfff (for Kharkiv). Wherever Russian rule reaches, Russian names follow. And if there is something that Russian rule especially likes, a shiny and easily perceived jewel, this something has to be labeled Russian, and be made part of the "Great Russian culture", since Russian culture is always unquestionably and non-negotiably Great. No one would dare say otherwise.

There is Catherine who is Great, and Peter who is Great, Great Russian literature, and the Great Russian ballet that the whole world must enjoy even if it takes an army of tanks to convince unbelievers.

Of course, if you ask a stranger somewhere on a busy London street what they personally consider great, it would probably not be a dead Russian monarch or a ballet dancer. They would name ice cream as something undoubtedly great. Perhaps a pint after work. A good movie, or a hug from a loved one on a warm summer night. It would probably not be Peter (unless it's the rabbit). "Great" is an evaluative category, a matter of taste. But what if you turn this uncertain notion—greatness—into unquestioned knowledge? Something repeated automatically because it'd been written it in a book so many times, or someone told you, or it is just a "common sense", because everyone knows.

---

18   June 2024, unpublished.

As I write these words, four guided bombs fall on Kharkiv, a city that is big but not great. Two people die instantly as a residential house is hit and a wall falls on a kitchen as the residents are having their weekend tea and reading. These victims will never be called great. The great Russian victims. Their human bodies are torn apart by pieces of metal dropped from a Soviet-era plane that a Russian pilot directs at a big city. This pilot, perhaps, also realizes the difference between great and big. He is fighting for the Great Russian world, or for a good salary to take home, to buy some decent vodka and fish once in a while. He kills people, but they don't belong to the Great Russian culture. And so, Peter the Great and Catherine the Great, and the Great Russian writer Alexander Pushkin are standing behind the pilot as he goes for another round. Perhaps, Alexandr Pushkin would support this pilot; after all, he hailed Peter's destruction of the Finnish settlements where today's St. Petersburg stands.

I have always wondered what it is that makes things great. From my school's program in Ukrainian history, I know that Catherine the Great dismantled the last traces of Ukrainian statehood, and enslaved the free settlers who'd come to Kharkiv from the west of today's Ukraine. The lands they'd once bought for cheap became a trap—"дешева рибка та погана юшка"—as my mom says, "cheap fish makes bad broth". These farmers became the serfs of Catherine's favorite people—military men who won her more territory in a plethora of imperial conquests. Catherine broke the agreement with the settlers of Kharkiv and enslaved them, and so, to my taste, she ain't that great.

The Russian pilot's number of victims rises to fifteen. Voltaire was duly paid for his adoration of Catherine. By Catherine surely, and from the taxes she got from my ancestors whom she'd enslaved. And then of course there's Peter. The guy behind the most horrible massacre of Ukrainian elites, the first of many—known as the Rape of Baturin. Baturin was the Ukrainian capital in baroque times, a vibrant young center of Ukrainian culture, like Kharkiv in the 1920s when Khvylovy wrote about it. Hopeful, not great. If I were to make my own judgment of Peter, the Russian tsar, "great" would probably not be the word I'd choose.

The Kharkiv River breathes in tiny waves, and I move a little bit away from the sun that slowly takes over the bench on which I'm writing these thoughts down.

The first photographs of the attack appear on social networks. I recognize the bus station. A ten-minute walk from my bench. The Great Russian culture is ever so close. Maybe that is why the world accepts its lethal judgements of taste? I return to Khvylovy—still the most stereotypical Kharkivian, reading a Kharkiv writer on the bank of the Kharkiv River. Khvylovy is holding a gun, in his text. He walks the city, exhausted from a heavy spring shower, and tries to imagine the places and people his gun had passed through before landing in his pocket. At some point the gun seems as alive as the man carrying it, as the city that, Khvylovy writes, "holds many tragedies and murders in its crooked paths and turns".

Hunger and the sun finally chase me off the bench. As I walk along the river, the summer heat is dry and unaffected, rolling out occasional wind whirls from the Wild Field. The café founded by my friend, who had to flee Kharkiv and will never return, is serving weekend picnic plates, kombucha, and spicy Vietnamese ice cream (created at a local Barabashova market by members of the Vietnamese diaspora). I opt for a healthy shawarma and a cold drink with coffee. Three dead, two children in the hospital. A very strange round building, one we used to call the Death Star, crumpled like a Christmas ornament under an explosive wave. A trolleybus passenger died on the spot. I finish my lunch and make a picture of a quirky rabbit on an old Soviet plate, bought by my friend at a Sunday flea market one day many winters ago.

A family of otters living in a pipe under the bridge over the Kharkiv River, are hiding, like everyone, from the afternoon sun as I walk back to the center to hear a lecture on comic books, in a literary apartment that once belonged to Yuri Shevelov. He is our biggest treasure (by "our", I mean Kharkivians). Despite his tremendous scholarship on the linguistic roots of old Ukrainian, Belarusian and Russian, he remains simply our "grandpa Yuri Shevelov", as a stencil on the wall of Rymarska Street calls him. Too close and too familiar to ever be great.

I walk up the stairs and join the lecture at Shevelov's apartment. Sitting in front of me is Anton Vusyk, a director at Nafta Theatre. In 2022 he produced a play, *Rainbow on Saltivka*, imagining the post-war future of his native district, levelled by Russian artillery. He is now reserving a seat for his wife, a touching gesture, on an armchair in the corner of Shevelov's room.

Twenty-eight in hospital, four in serious condition. One Russian bomb achieved greatness.

Coming here, I walk up a narrow descent and take a picture of a three-colored tabby against street art by Hamlet Zinkivsky, the main local celebrity artist, whose dominion over the cityscape is constantly disputed by every other artist. Kharkiv's acid humor will not allow him to become great. I'm going to post the cat on Twitter, saying that's what Zinkivsky really looks like.

The number of injured has risen to thirty-eight.

Yaryna Tsymbal, the scholar of 1920s Ukrainian fiction and a brilliant explorer of precious genre novels about Kharkiv, is sitting in the first row at the lecture, delivered by the younger Boris Filonenko (we specify this as his father is himself a well-known philosopher). The younger Boris curated the Ukrainian pavilion at the 2022 Venice Biennale, helping Mavlo Makov ship *The Fountain of Exhaustion* from Kharkiv to Italy, in the middle of a refugee crisis across the flooded Polish border. Today he is talking about Ukrainian comic books. The moderator, Mykola Kolomyets, was a promising young artist when the war started in 2014. He has made only one work since, focusing on teaching children instead. These two are resolutely cool. in a way it's better than great, because it's easier to talk to cool people.

The Great Russian ballet continues to dominate Ukrainian ballet schools thanks to an old Soviet textbook written for use in all the ethnic republics. Most of the teachers still speak Russian, as they were sent to these republics from Russia to teach their indigenous population the art of raising a leg and enduring acute pain, and to judge, by measuring the shape of their skulls, whether they were apt to perform a good twirl.

Sitting to my right at the lecture is Nina Khyzhna, another director at Nafta Theater. She doesn't have a ballet education, work instead with the free movement of the body, and her latest play, *Someone Like Me*, is dedicated to expressing personal experience of the war through motion, anarchic and ever-changing. I'm glad she doesn't dance in *Swan Lake*.

Boris Filonenko starts to speak about the 1920s artist Vasyl Yermilov, who imagined a whole city of the future made out of plywood, and how today our city speaks of its wounds through the pieces of plywood covering broken windows. Yermilov gave us Kharkivians some avant-garde thinking, but he didn't become Great like Kazimir Malevich. Yermilov was scared by the murder of half of his friends in the 1930s, became a modest teacher of art, and did not speak of the past to anyone till the end of his life. It was a broken generation, made up of those who would never become Great. Perhaps for the best, since Malevich has been appropriated as a Great Russian artist, hanging in world museums, a victim of the Russian love of greatness. Greedily, we get to keep Yermilov, our secret genius, to ourselves.

Because a friend asked me to, today I opened a fundraiser for the army, adorned with a rainbow flag as it's Kyiv Pride month. Other LGBTQ friends from abroad cover the entire sum, 2,000 hryvnias, in two hours as the number of bus station victims rises from eighteen to thirty-eight. It still feels like a risk to support LGBTQ in Ukraine, but that's the society I aspire to see.

To my left, Tetyana Pylypchuk, the Kharkiv literary museum director, sits listening to a talk about Ukrainian comic books. The museum has been slowly excavating the past, uncovering forgotten names and the archives of Kharkiv's executed and oppressed writers. I particularly like the legacy of Yuri Shovkipkyas, who wrote short detective stories about Dr. Piddubnyi, who once saw a body fall from Derzhprom, the first modernist skyscraper in Ukraine. He also wrote a novel about doctors and love triangles, a 1950s *Grey's Anatomy* of sorts. His books are not great nor genius, but the sheer pleasure of pulp fiction, the kind you get to read soaking in the bathtub after a long busy day.

I like that the literary museum does not discriminate between great literature and pulp fiction, since my taste in books is often bizarre and I develop infatuations with texts no one else would look at twice.

My friend sends a picture of Serhii Zhadan posing at 7 Sklad, a hipster food market ten minutes away from Shevelov's apartment. In his leather jacket, Zhadan is enjoying a weekend break away from his new military career. Zhadan is our one chance at getting a Nobel Prize, some say. Infuriatingly, he doesn't want to write the Great Ukrainian Novel, preferring to live and write poetry and pretend to be a 1990s rock star at hipster food markets.

In the row in front of me I notice an academic who once made me so angry that I dashed out of the room and never returned and never spoke to him again. That was definitely not a great experience, I'd say. I like that I could speak my mind to anyone in this room if I chose and that the secret police would not take me away for doing so. Generations of persistent, not great, Ukrainians slowly pushed for and gained this freedom.

I am trying to write a smart analysis of the concept of Russian greatness and how it is used in creating the hierarchies of lives under its imperial gaze. But every time I try to write about Russia, I end up writing about Ukraine. And so, instead, I am writing about this day, so suffocatingly hot and tragic and beautiful. I want to write about these people living around me just this second. About the three people who died ten minutes away from my bench. The woman killed walking out of the trolleybus had pink platform sandals, which can be seen under the blanket covering her on a picture in social networks. Her friend would later post that the woman in pink sandals, Kateryna, wasn't meant to get down at that stop. She was only helping an old lady with her trolley bag. Kateryna died, helping a stranger. Her friend wrote that they liked taking long walks across the city to the Central Park where they ate fried Crimean Tatar meat pies, "Chibereki", with champagne.

I can't seem to make myself write about the Great Russian culture, as, instead, I want to talk about melting concrete and the sun's rays piercing the single surviving wall of a nineteenth-century ruin on the Kharkiv River. About the fisherman there. In his 1920s short story, Khvylovy writes about the river bank, where fishermen, too, are trying to catch something in the dirty waters of this very river. Like me, Khvylovy naively thinks of the fishermen as the sole remnants of the past. These fishermen will outlive us both. As I walk along the Kharkiv River, a fisherman, with a rod and his jeans rolled up, climbs over an ornamented fence and walks across the flowerbed, then strolls down the sidewalk, his flip flops leaving wet prints on the pavement. The overpriced city paving stones fit together perfectly and display the uneven marks of the river water dragged by the flip flops. The fisherman fades into the horizon, walking towards the bridge under which a white otter family lives. He may well live there too.

The lecture about comic books is rolling to a close as Filonenko says that he does not approve of our constant desire to get out of our bubble. Stay in it, he says, enjoy the bubble, swim in it and study its close intensity, the densely populated beauty of your social bubble. One of my neighbors sighs and covers her face with her hands, exhausted from the stuffy hot air in the room that once belonged to Yuri Shevelov. I finish this essay with words of love for our shrunken wartime bubbles. In this war, Kharkiv is one, a city where death stalks writers as they write, or even if, like Serhii Zhadan, they don't write their great Nobel prizewinning novels.

In the 1928 Venice Biennale, the Kharkiv artists Vasyl Sedlar and Ivan Padalka were presented in a separate department in the Soviet pavilion reserved for "Ukrainian artists". They did not live far from Shevelov. They all lived somewhere near, our congenial non-great Ukrainian artists.

Kharkiv, "a city big, but not great", can accommodate literary lectures and civilian deaths in a period of two hours and in an area of three square kilometers. I come back to this phrase often now. Khvylovy safeguarding Kharkiv as a city that can't be Russian, because it isn't Great. I thank Khvylovy for that, even if he meant something else. Kharkiv might be great to us, but that greatness is not the kind one shouts about; it's our small social bubble's quiet adoration, whispered on a stuffy evening in June 2024.

Inspired by the fisherman, I buy a pair of flip flops, so comfortable I could probably escape a great Russian bomb in them.

They are black and white, like this war. The day and the text are rolling to its refreshing close. Fifty-two injured. A family of entrepreneurs survives by stepping out to enjoy a cup of coffee on their lunch break, when their shop is obliterated by a Russian pilot. Walking to the metro just before the curfew I take a selfie with the Opera House in the background. I suddenly feel that I don't have enough photographs of myself in this big fragile city. I am fine with the picture not being Great.

In the Exploding Silence[19]

1.

One day in the second year of the war I woke up to silence. The ground beneath my newly constructed five-story was not vibrating with the movement of heavy military vehicles. When I opened the window, the gray morning leaked in, smelling of fireworks and hope. I rushed to the balcony and observed the outskirts of the city — the burnt forest, a pair of ruined high rises, and the bomb-damaged menorah on the World War II Jewish memorial. Quiet and serene. The war is over, I thought.

But the war was far from over. In the days to come missiles flew and crashed into the playgrounds, buildings, and roads around my house, leaving five-meter craters around cars and rented electric scooters. Neither my street nor the city itself can really be called flat any longer, I thought, taking out a tiny bag of plastic rubbish. The air raid sirens screamed when a missile entered the city's air space as I was walking to the water fountain where my street intersected with a tiny park. Explosions were recorded and published on Twitter, and I watched them, like all the world, with the detached aseptic air of a video game observer. The war went on. But, for some reason, I could not hear the explosions anymore.

My physician, a terrifyingly tall serene statue of a woman, said that something was wrong with "either my head or my ears", which sounded about right. Aren't ears part of the head anyway? The only thing we both agreed on during the dry ten-minute video call conducted from the safety of my bathtub, behind the two comfortable walls of my newly painted perfectly white flat, was that losing the ability to hear explosions in such a precarious time could pose "additional discomfort for my mental wellbeing".

The first thing I learnt, when the city was surrounded, in the early days of March the year before, was the art of reading the explosions. I learnt to tell "incoming" from "outgoing" fire, theirs

---

[19] 2022, Unpublished.

from ours. Our fire was dim, a loud puff of smoke from a pipe, as though Gandalf the Grey were emerging from the very soil. Enemy fire was sharp as a knife that cut through your body. Car alarms would go off, and the walls of the flat would dance, celebrating a new addition of scorched metal to the neighborhood ecosystem.

When the enemy was pushed back slightly, new sounds were added, rare and beautiful, air defense ripping apart an enemy missile in the sky, or a series of laser *pius* hunting a deadly drone, turning us into spectators at a live *Star Trek* movie set. But almost instantly the enemy learnt a new trick too. Repurposing air defense missiles, they started to fire them at us, old Soviet rust that wasn't supposed to be precise or kind. Like my mom's Soviet teachers.

When these old Soviet teachers flew at the city, it was like Russian roulette. I would sit in the hallway, in torchlight and drinking a cup of chamomile tea with special health-enhancing enzymes and vitamin B, and read the messages as they came: "ANOTHER FLIES"; "ONE MORE IN THE AIR"; "HIDE"; "A-HOLE HIT THE SCHOOL". Four, six or eight blasts would follow, always an even number in the old brotherly Slavic tradition—an even number of roses for the dead. Ten minutes when my muscles cemented the stress in a knot of nauseating fear that not even chamomile tea could soothe. I started to breathe again when new messages appeared: "YOU CAN THROW AWAY THE WET NAPPIES NOW. ALL CLEAR".

I learnt the grammar of explosions, the missile economy, even if there was no point in hiding. Forty seconds wasn't enough to get from my shiny new bathtub to the cellar. I learnt to pay attention to the sirens, and then I learnt to ignore the sirens. Humans, the most adaptable animals on Earth, can live and die in any climate.

The first night of winter was the first night that I didn't hear an explosion. I stared at the ceiling—with dry sleepless eyes (despite what the Magnesium sedative supplement producer promised)—until the blush of apricot dawn touched the fractured facade of a primary school across the road. Snow started to fall. I walked out and saw a line of cat paw tracks on the sidewalk. It wasn't cold, but the snow refused to melt. Community services were replacing the glass at the bus stop across the road from a gas station that had been bombed.

My odyssey into a world where things blew up silently, seen out of the corner of the eye, on the fringes of newspapers and messaging services, and in poorly edited YouTube videos, marked the coming of the cold. I lost what little comfort I had. I could not count the blasts, I could not tell when a raid would start, my muscles had trouble relaxing as I was never sure when the explosions were over. The silence was getting to me like a quiet methodical serial killer. The silence was very patient.

Winter was wrapped in the hectic buzz of petroleum generators outside shops and cafés. Power stations were targeted, set on fire. Luckily I had two power banks and lots of blankets from grandma's village hut. In her late years she weaved colorful *kotsy*, heavy mixed wool and linen carpets you could throw over your shoulders to look like the big bad wolf from the fairy tale.

All my close relatives had left the city. My furry winter backpack—water- but not missile-resistant—chimed with key chains when I walked down the metro escalator, hurrying to get to everyone's flat to check on their flowers and collect their electricity bills, to make sure that potential robbers knew the places were inhabited, and to pick new books to read. I would take the old Soviet books for recycling, slowly replacing them with 1960s poetry, so that, if my relatives ever came back, they would live in new, poetic and very Ukrainian rooms. The old Soviet books would help raise funds for sniper's night vision scope. My relatives would never return.

My graphic designer work suffered especially badly in January after a full week's blackout. An LA gaming company didn't get their logo in time for a potential investor presentation, and gave me a long talk on the virtue of being vigilant and more invested in the company's success, the three of them smiling with perfect mouths of teeth, the work of the same dentist with an office overlooking palm trees, I hoped.

Things improved after New Year, when slowly, like the first snowdrops, familiar cafés started to reopen, and I was able to sit down with a cooling cup of coffee, drawing intricate circles and waves in the vignettes of professional websites. I fell in love with the smooth lines. The winter thaw was gentle and pretty in the Wild Field, the endless flatlands. One day the snow suddenly melted, and the streets were all drowned in sugary slush. And the land, like the lines on the websites I drew, grew smooth and elegant.

2.

At an IT class, at school waiting for my turn on the computer, I once closed my eyes and wished that all the people would disappear, so that I could play video games, walk the streets and look into every house of the city. Sometimes I think that maybe I was the one who brought the war here, that I am to blame, that stupid wish imagined the war into reality.

My physician returned from abroad, this time conducting a dry ten-minute consultation in person. Tapping my knees did not contribute much to understanding my selective deafness, and I left the stuffy dark office, windows covered in plywood, with a familiar feeling of disorientation. As the metro froze in a power outage, I walked home through many different cities—bombed and untouched—plastered together with spit and a chewing gum. Central Street was blinking at me with its elegant art nouveau windows, shattered, glass teeth adorning the frames. I passed the bicycle bridge (where the famous bicycle factory never properly worked). The houses grew newer and duller, and by the time my neighborhood started in a massive conglomeration of plants, the Soviet nine-story buildings looked almost more interesting in their new fractured form, silhouettes embracing the red horizon, varied, the scars and amputations varying their uniform box-like shape.

The busiest spot in the area was the local supermarket. Once hit by an S-300 missile, it swiftly grew back with new aluminum walls. In the ready-meal department, the respectable, white-aproned shop assistant typically ignored my looking at the salads. Feeling awkward, I migrated to the fruit to stare at a mountain of withered oranges and wrinkly apples. The shop assistant, a young man in a blue and yellow T-shirt and an apron so fresh the assistant must have been born that very day, ran up to help. His enthusiasm reeked of a hopeful dreamer of the supermarket hierarchy.

'Your apron hasn't gone through the frozen food department yet,' I noted. The guy laughed and said he'd worked there for a month, and was happy simply because we were alive and had food and all that somehow made us get through the day.

The rest of the evening flew by fast. The broadband was fixed, and all the season 25 *MasterChef* episodes had to be watched. Around ten I went to the kitchen to put the kettle on.

When I returned, shards of glass covered the glitzy surface of my white Scandinavian desk, making it bizarrely even more chic, an avant-garde Bauhaus product. The curtains danced, swooshing glass across the room, and somewhere a violent ray of electric light made a circle like a rainbow across the horizon:

"All right?"
"Alive?"
"How are you, dear?"
"Is everything quiet?"
"Why aren't you picking up the goddamn phone????"
"What's up, kid?"

Messages lit up in a symphony of distant concern. "Fine. I did not hear anything," I copypasted back.

The kettle screamed a high opera note. My perfect wood board floor, the color of "young birch", glistened with the tiny diamonds from my new "European" windows.

3.

It took Pan[20] Ihor forty minutes to drive from the village in his old German beetle, a stack of plywood on the roof. He had fixed a thousand windows in the city, and cleverly preferred to live in a lake house far away. We'd called him for help in the flats of my other relatives. He joked that with such luck I would live to a hundred.

When the big war began, we all lost our patronymics and became "Pan" and "Pani". The war made our names comfortably shorter, our language more efficient.

---

20 *Pan/Pani*, a polite way to address a person in Ukrainian.

"Maybe we are no longer defined by the actions of our fathers to use patronymics." — he said.

We shook hands like two brokers at a stock exchange, and the beetle swooshed its way to other lucky homeowners. A Latvian NGO supplied him with materials and gas money.

4.

"I will live to a hundred, not a day less and not a day more", my second uncle Hena used to say. Like most Ukrainian men in the 1990s, he was an alcoholic, but a humorous one, unlike my other alcoholic uncle, who was sad and always depressed. We would play endless games of chess with Uncle Hena, and he would let me win every third one.

He died at fifty-four on a cold train to Moscow, and who knows what the hell he was even doing there, but it took us a lot of effort to get his body back, and the gravediggers, two teenagers, had a blast chiseling frozen soil on a Christmas Eve. Uncle Hena knew how to entertain the younger generation.

Unlike Uncle Hena, I jogged every morning, did fifty pushups before lunch and allowed myself a single semi-dry cider once a week. Unlike Uncle Hena, I never really wanted to live to a hundred.

On one of the last warm January evenings I was walking with Sahko, the happy supermarket consultant, from his work. The station on the other side of the highway was waiting for one last bus to depart to the little town where Sashko lived and where another of my uncles, surprisingly also an alcoholic, used to be a test pilot in his former and (I hope) soberer life.

We wandered around the bus stop, moving to keep warm.

The grave of an unknown Soviet soldier was hiding in the bushes.

"Why didn't they take them back?", Sashko asked. "The soldiers who stayed in our ground?"

"Maybe they thought the Soviets would be here forever?"

"I'm not talking about the Soviets. I mean today, the invaders. Remember a tank drove down here on the first day?", he asked.

"What tank?" I fixed my gaze on Sashko, and took the opportunity to notice he had a very strange shade of hazel in his eyes, and his skin was so perfect that he could model facial care products on TikTok.

"When they broke through, it was only one tank, and it didn't make it to the center. But I'm still wondering what happened to the crew. I couldn't find any news either from the police or the newspapers. As if that tank crew melted into thin air." Sashko was about to add something, but the bus driver had finally finished his cigarette and asked the passengers to get inside. Since Sashko was one of the three passengers, he hurried to kiss me goodbye.

5.

Perhaps, had the lovely cheerful Sashko never told me about the tank, I would have passed the little park between the bus stop and my house like I always did, engulfed in my own thoughts and the failures at work. But it was a strange evening, and the moon swam up the sky, violently honest, and with this moon I suddenly imagined a line of enemy soldiers moving through the air, like the Wild Hunt in the old Lithuanian fairytale about King Stakh. My own sick imagination made the branches under my feet sharp and prickly like hunters' arrows, or Soviet soldiers' medals. I tripped and fell.

There, just a spit away from the park path between the highway and my house, I saw it. A male hand was looking out of the ground, through dry leaves and twisted beer cans. The skin was almost as gray as the cans' aluminum. The fingernail on the pinky had slid off and was hanging, unnaturally, like a bad Christmas ornament. Overall, it was quite clear that, whether attached to a body or separate, the hand was very much dead. The pattern of dots on the cuff of the invader's military uniform seemed the only thing that kept the hand in the air.

The rain started, heavy like a wet mattress. But for me the entire world shrank to a hand. Or was it really a branch adorned with fingernails? The hand, the hand, the word itself grew weirder as I repeated it in my head. Language is strange. When you slow down and start to think, it melts away from your brain, and soon, more and more slowly, a primordial humdrum replaces it. Monsters rise from under the silence of the fallen.

The word and the hand grew through the rain, washed with the water. I did not feel alone, because the hand was staring at me. Even as I stood up and walked, entering my home, shaking, through the darkness of the hallway, from behind the door, from behind the trees, the hand was watching me.

The red and black ribbon of the invading army, a Georgian ribbon, a symbol of genocide, dangled torn at the edges and bloodied, and left marks on the new carpet I'd purchased at a Danish furniture shop. I woke up, shook my head, jumped on one leg and then the other to make the image to disappear. There were no missiles through the night, no alarms, but for some reason I went to sleep in the bathtub anyway. I like the repeated routine of weaving a nest out of two winter blankets with the *kots* carpet on top, in case the tiles started to fall (they were badly fixed in the first place).

From under my bathtub the sound came. A very quiet cough. I decided it was a gust of air.

6.

The hand became my silent companion for the explosions that I couldn't hear. In February, Sashko got two tickets to the opera. He won them in a secret silent charity auction, the kind where they send you the address one hour before the event for safety reasons, even if we all knew that only one place could hold that many people. The alien ship of the modernist opera house had grown raw and creaky after a year of silence, and the singers themselves seemed to make an effort to be quieter than usual, wary of the missile launcher operators on the other side of the border.

Brass candelabras and side lights in the style of *Doctor Who* led to an underground ladies' room that belonged in a provincial bus station, not merely for the graffiti drawn with black eyeliner of every quality. Beethoven profiles mixed with phone numbers and obscenities.

"You also feel this is the safest place now?", a teenage girl in punk-like torn tights and a polyurethane beret asked as we washed our hands in the sinks' icy water.

I did feel safer in the underground nooks, rooms and cellars of the grand Opera. Climbing to the second balcony felt like asking to be bombed. Oblivious in the eternal happiness of a young life, Sashko was recording the play, smiling like a Shiba puppy. It was a shatteringly beautiful performance we all felt could be our last, which made the singers work above and beyond the price tag. The proceeds went to demining equipment, which felt gratifying, almost worth the danger.

7.

The night city, mysterious in its wartime dangerous charm, with human presences lurking in the dark, had a sobering effect on the way back from the concert. Sashko's scarf, as he wrapped it around me, smelled of wax candles. I wasn't cold, he knew; it was just a nervous gesture, caring for another body. Were we even allowed to enjoy life with all the war around? As Sashko chirruped with delight, his beautiful cheekbones rimy with pink rainbows of frost, I felt sad. The dead hand of the enemy soldier overshadowed living beauty, a sudden smell of rotten mince made me breathe through my mouth.

The traffic light beamed an envious green and as I took a step onto the perfectly smooth road, my shoe slipped, and I flew. In the brief moment of flight, before Sashko hot dry hand caught me, I saw the blue dead hand waltz like a snowflake from above. Boots, old and worn out, looted from a World War II memorial museum, appeared before my eyes too. Cars hurried past, impatient to get home before the curfew, honking, skirting me, as I stood there looking at the old military boots of the dead soldier floating in the air.

A voice, bitterly sarcastic, cut through the cold wind. I hate it when people whisper in my ear, even close friends. What to say of the invaders.

"They all left", the voice croaked in his language, sharp and glassy, the invader's accent, in which everything sounds like an eternal "aaaa". "Why then did you stay in your dying city? Everyone in the world knows that we will finish you. You are almost gone. Erased. Your city will never have existed".

Sashko picked me up by the hand, gently, as he would lift a crate of wine at the supermarket.

"Are you fine?", he asked.

"So-so", I answered, making Sashko frown, as he wasn't used to pessimists.

"We will blind them with our money, our oil and our ballet dancers, and they'll forget you like they forgot the others. We will grind your bones into the dust of the road. A soldier like me will write a book for a famous publisher, and people in airports will devour our words, like they always do. And no one will remember you existed. The dust of your bones and your blood will be mixed into the paper of our new books. In a century we'll raise Olympic stadiums over your bones. In the empty field where your city once stood".

This time, I knew the dead soldier's words were lies, no more than his intentions when he crossed the border that February night, before someone shot his tank, before he was buried in a shallow grave. Or, rather, I hoped they were just that. Shashko helped me to finally cross the road and we breathed the freshness of the winter air, smiling as though we did not see the cardboard covering the blown-out windows of the bombed houses we passed on the way to the metro. Someone painted flowers on the cardboard, naive and childish, like Sashko's optimism and beautiful eyes.

"Everyone's a bit on edge these days," Sashko said as we walked through the empty metro train. When the metro is empty it feels as if you're flying through the dark tunnels, swift and fragile.

8.

"Try not to watch the news, read a romance novel. In these times no pills will help," the psychotherapist counselled convincingly when he saw me in the free clinic the next morning. He was one of those state doctors who make you understand why my unaffected private therapist was worth the coin. Most private doctors either evacuated or went to the front, while mine had simply disappeared in the humdrum of the war. As I collected the thin notepad with all the histories of all my childhood diseases, a man walked in, and the therapist lost interest in me, invested instead in a small scheme involving receipts for those seeking to avoid mobilization. It was not even ten in the morning when I walked out of the hospital door with a prescription for a dietary supplement and a pack of herbal tea.

In order to get home, I would have to pass the shallow grave of the dead Russian soldier. I no longer felt it was my neighborhood. It was his now. Fear riddled and occupied the dark corners of its streets. I had not slept in my bed for months, instead spending my nights in jeans and laced Doc Martens in my bathtub. Everything became uncomfortable—my city, my new flat, and my new Martens alike.

Drifting without purpose was the most tedious activity. I went to the cinema. A three-hour-long movie, miraculously uninterrupted by an air raid siren, finished at two. The skeletons of art deco windows breathed the air, in and out along the central street. Five explosions killed a kid near the football stadium as I crossed the bicycle bridge, cursing the pain from my shoes. I felt as if I lived in the margins of a book. When everyone follows the plot, I sink into blind corners. A photo of a child dead in his bed covered by a peony blanket flooded social networks.

I jumped into the metro. I couldn't say I was scared, but I honestly could not walk the streets and pretend that the city still belonged to us after all the things they were allowed to do to it.

9.

Choosing a cordless lamp felt important faced with the promised inevitable nuclear meltdown. I roamed the Danish furniture store, miraculously open, on the second floor of the supermarket. By the cashiers a basketful of awkwardly sewn gnomes rested, their cone hats hiding half of their faces to save on the eye buttons. I grabbed one that looked particularly clumsy, with one leg shorter than the other, and laid it on the counter.

"You should buy his girlfriend too, really", the shop assistant said in a tone that did not tolerate objection. "Standing there at your house all alone? He'll go mad. With only ten left, you would never find him a mate if you change your mind".

"Fine, I'm not a monster!", I admitted, more to myself than to the shop assistant. I tried to find a girl with similar factory defects, but all the girl gnomes looked like Hollywood stars. I grabbed the one at the back, and finally left the furniture department feeling slightly ridiculous but satisfied, having saved a family of inanimate objects.

Sashko walked around the fruit department, as always disproportionally pedantic and cheerful, sorting oranges of the first category by size and shape so as to build the most perfect pyramid before a lady snatched two from the bottom, and the construction collapsed, spraying expensive natural citrus fumes over the slippery floor.

"These should go on sale now", he said, no anger in his voice, collecting the damaged oranges as I walked up.

"I know that you will take them. You always pick the poor ones. Wait till I change the price tag".

"I have all the time in the world tonight", I answered.

"Funny, so do I, since we're supposed to close", Sashko smiled, as if he really loved his work. "Could you just wait by the entrance and make sure no one walks in?"

When I got to the sliding door, the night guard had already switched the lights off. In the dark my heartbeat was loud.

I suddenly remembered hugging mom goodbye, when the evacuation train arrived at the platform.

"I love you," I said.

"Is it because you don't have anybody else to love?", Mom asked. She did not mean it, was too tired and irritated because of the crowd. But, every once in a while, the vicious melody of her words rose up in my head instead of the explosions that sparkled in the horizon somewhere downtown, on a street with art nouveau windows.

I didn't have anything to love. Nothing but the walls of the tiny new apartment, purchased on a whim, in the face of piling loans. I don't know why I didn't want to leave when the war finally rumbled into the city on the tanks and in the armored vehicles of the invading soldiers. I couldn't muster the thought that someone else, an enemy, would live in my tiny apartment, surrounded by my perfectly white walls and Charlie Chaplin posters. That they would cook in my stylish gray kitchen, covered in the expensive paint that lets you write daily wishes with chalk. My bathroom tiles, the color of pale lemons, my bathtub, black, as I'd always dreamt of, my deathless orchid that started to crawl out of its pot to strangle me. These were the things I thought I loved enough to risk a life for.

I thought about it walking to the sliding doors, and laughter cut me in half. All for this, to become a stranger in that flat because of some dead soldier, not even a live one, not one who would drag dirt over my heated white marble floors.

10.

The dead soldier was standing there on the other side of the supermarket door, looking at me from the dark. In the lonely light from the parking streetlight, his shadow cut through the blackness of the park. He was beating the door with fists half eaten by insects, heat and cold. Unable to cross the threshold, since the sliding door only reacted to living people, the dead soldier spat at the glass, a dark liquid from a deep Siberian bog.

"You won," I laughed, unable to calm down. "You chased me out of my home, what else do you want?" I stepped up and spat at the glass from the inside. My spit was clear, frothy, and did not mix with the dead soldier's.

The door did not slide open. Not for the dead soldier, not for me.

11.

"You will never hear your missile", they said. "The one that kills you will come in silence".

When I stopped hearing explosions, I thought that the city was broken. But standing at the closed door of the supermarket, I had to agree with my mother, however cruel she may sometimes have been. I stayed because I had no one and nothing else to love but the tiny new apartment. I valued it so much I would have let the missile launcher operators of the invading army bury me in it.

The world did not stop when I realized that I had not survived the war. No one survives the war, neither the living nor the dead. In a way we all perish, beautiful art deco houses with intricate windows, and poor lonely girls in cheap residential area flats built of sticks and stones with walls as thin as painted cardboard.

The only thing that made me mad was the dead soldier, still lying in my ground, his slime sliding down the perfectly clean glass doors of the supermarket.

"Why are you still here?!", I shouted in his language. The words came slowly, as I hadn't spoken that language for a long time. The enemy soldier said nothing, but continued to gnaw at the door, pointless as it was. We were left forever there in the vicious circle of fighting for my land.

12.

Was it my apartment where it all happened? That time when the windows got blown out? Or the supermarket? Was it the theater? I knew I shouldn't have attended public events in precarious times. But it could well have been that one time, in the early days, when I went to fetch water from a well behind rows of rusty garages. The memories were crumbling in my head, shrinking like discounted apples. It was all of those places in the end.

"I'm protecting my home, my new curtains and my angry orchid. What are *you* doing here?", I asked the dead man.

The head looked up quickly, and his right ear started to slide down his neck.

"They sent the best ones for the reckoning, I bet. You grew up in a family of professional soldiers. Your dad was cutting off Chechen heads in the nineties, firing on the market in Grozny. Uncle disappeared somewhere in Kandahar, and, of course, grandpa, the big deal in Stalin's punishment battalions brought you gold watches from the rubble of Berlin. I bet you still keep the loot in a well-polished family chest".

The siren started to howl, the third rooster before dawn. It took a long time to explain to the corpse of a dead soldier the futility of its existence. The night was slowly receding, not unlike his flesh.

When the first customer, an elderly lady, pulled a rolling bag towards the door ten minutes before opening, her heavy breath knocking at the sliding glass door in the blushing sun, the invader had melted into a pool of slushy snow under her determined feet.

Sashko, accustomed to the drill, came up and shouted, "It's ten to eight!!!" And walked away, picking up a bag with two gnomes that someone had lost the night before.

Our eyes did not meet. Sashko was busy doing his living chores, pale and monotonous in the day's first innocent hours in the big empty city.

13.

There's nothing more magical than a brisk walk through the old wild park as the snow is melting. The shallow grave of the invading soldier was covered in red police tape. Journalists had reported the find, but no one cared to investigate who may have put the body there.

I walked to my yard, sat on the swings, the middle section broken by a young vandal on the fourth floor. The metal beams of the swing squealed, coats of rusty paint peeling with each swing.

Fresh windows had been installed in my flat. Black panes like I'd always wanted. The new owners brought a stroller down the elevator. I was happy for them having the means to buy pretty things.

I looked at the windows and went past the house, behind the yard to the last buildings of the city, past a cigarette factory, and a cattle farm, and away like Skovoroda, a wandering Ukrainian philosopher of the Baroque.

My heart became light. I could go anywhere, knowing that I would never hear explosions ever again. Winter wouldn't last forever.

Outro to "In the Exploding Silence"

In the summer of 2022 I was staying in my parents' apartment on the outskirts of Kharkiv. The Russian military had just repurposed S-300 missiles (normally used for air defense) to attack the city. Throughout August, every night at 1 or 2 a.m, two, four or six S-300 missiles landed on Kharkiv, exploding loudly, sometimes pleasingly far, at other times making car alarms below my bedroom window wail. I became so used to this schedule that, despite being an early bird, I couldn't go to sleep before hearing the explosions. Then, one night in late August, no S-300 struck. Although it was the first quiet night in the whole of the summer, it was in a way the worst night. I lay awake till dawn, waiting for the explosion that never came. I was later told that the Germans used this tactic in World War II. Sometime around dawn, I started questioning my own mind. Had the explosion happened, and I failed to notice it, or, even worse, had I been killed – because you never hear "your" missile, as the saying has it. It was exquisite torture.

I started writing the story during those waking hours, slipping into doubt and insanity. Some of the events in it are factual. The concert in the Kharkiv Opera House, full of people, was real. I remember women laughing, as they refreshed their red lipstick in the toilet, that we could be bombed at any moment. True is the bizarre homeliness of Kharkiv despite its crumbling exterior. The supermarket is the bombed supermarket near my metro station. Locals joked that it was bombed because of the huge Ukrainian flag on its facade. It was rebuilt in a week, renamed "Kharkiv", with two additional flags at its entrance. The gnomes from the Jysk store were a meme of the first winter of the big war. People would post pictures of homely Christmas gnomes, writing "another Shaheed drone night" or "I'm not afraid of nukes anymore". I really appreciate that, unlike other international furniture retailers, Jysk remained in Ukraine, giving us a welcome respite, satisfying our shopaholic tendencies to cope with reality. The gnomes stand on my piano now. Things I never use should cling to each another. The body in the park is also real. Though, after the initial news, I never found a follow-up of who that Russian soldier was, what he was doing in our district, or where his body ended up. If David Lynch had been Ukrainian, that would have fascinated him. The graves to unknown Russian soldiers from World War II are also still there, still tended by the *remaining employees in the factory. In 2022 I sneaked into the factory museum in a building that had been bombed and took photos of the letters the museum workers received from Russia, asking about the remains of their relatives. All of the glass in that building had fallen out and broken, and I remember unbelievably fat stray dogs crunching their way over half a meter of shredded glass. The dogs are still being fed by the night watchmen in the bombed factory. Finally, I feel that I really did die the summer that I first came to Kharkiv to transition into that new reality. Not all of me, but that innocence only people never touched by war experience, the naive and kind version of you. I miss it sometimes. The innocent naivety of peace. But this new version feels more honest, the new wartime Kharkiv and me, we made peace with each other, and that is also important for someone who stays in it for the long run.*

This story is a fantasy, but, in a way, it is truer than all the nonfiction I've ever written.

Afterword

A couple of miles from the archeological site of the ancient Donets settlement, just outside of Kharkiv, there is the small township of Pokotylivka. The central park of Pokotylivka houses a monument to the Soviet partisans, to Holodomor, a monument to the people killed during Stalin's repressions, a monument to Ivan Sirko (a legendary seventeenth-century Cossack), a monument to Chernobyl, and a monument to the defenders of Ukraine in the Anti-Terrorist Operation of 2014–2022, all peacefully coexisting. A giant Soviet star at the entrance to the park is draped with the blue and yellow Ukrainian flag. Locals say that, during the holidays, competing political parties — ex-communists, former SBU officers, and local mini-oligarchs — set up stages across from each other. The competing parties' blasting rhythms clash in the middle of the square, vying for an electorate of a hundred people. The sounds of these political battles travel down the valley till their echo settles in the remains of the old Donets town. Considering that centuries covered in our history books bear the title "interpersonal conflicts of Kyivan Rus", chances are that Donets wasn't much different from Pokotylivka.[21] And that is all you need to know about Ukraine.

You might notice, reading this book, that I haven't said much about the Russian people, the proverbial other side. I feel this absence too. Like all Ukrainians, I have been thinking about the Russian people a lot. A LOT.[22] Not about Vladimir Putin, whose motives and persona are quite banal and uninteresting. I leave him to Western polytology professors and their weird fantasies. Instead, I've been

---

21 The term "Kyivan Rus" is ahistorical, but it was used in our school history books, which parroted Soviet textbooks. The phrase first appeared after Moscow appropriated the name "Rus". In essence, Rus and Russia are two different political entities. Rus, more anarchic and horizonal, contains some things reminiscent of Ukrainian identity. Of course, Ukraine doesn't trade in slaves nor does it plan to attack Constantinople. So, we haven't inherited all the traits.

22 I don't mean the airline, being a Ryanair girl myself.

thinking about the people of Bilhorod, a city near to Kharkiv.[23] These particular people have often been on my mind. In the first days of the invasion Kharkiv's well-known Telegram channel, *Huyovyi Kharkiv*,[24] published a list of city channels and blogs that Bilhorod people used, as we once did, to share beauty parlor ads and sushi delivery phone numbers. Like many Kharkivians, I looked through these channels obsessively, fascinated by the nonchalant, almost placid mood that inhabited the Bolhorod community, only thirty kilometers from my bombed home. One video was particularly mesmerizing. In the dark of evening, Bilhorod locals stood near their cars and cheered the bright comets of S-300 missiles flying towards Kharkiv. I felt—not rage, since rage has been the usual background of my life since the full-scale invasion—but a genuine curiosity about their kind of people, their education, culture, what led them to being so deeply indifferent to the pain of others. Slowly, I began to understand that such behavior wasn't the work of a day.

In World War II Soviet people—Ukrainians included—were often similarly disaffected, devoid of a personal ethical standing that they would be willing to defend.[25] Elderly people in Kharkiv often told me that the Nazi occupation wasn't "much worse" ("than the Russian Soviet one"—something they would never dare declare, of course). They would smile, recalling that some German officers "gave them chocolates". They were kids back then; for many, it was their first taste of chocolate. The story was always repeated, and always sounded the same, sometimes concluding with a statement that never ceased to perplex me: "perhaps we would have lived better under the Germans. Look at their washing machines" (I'm not kidding, elderly people always mentioned either them or

---

23 I use "Bilhorod" rather than official Belgorod as a tongue-in-cheek reminder that this city was once pronounced the capital of Ukraine. Although the city's population had always been Russian (in contrast to the lands in the southern part of the region, which were historically Ukrainian), in 1918 the Ukrainian hetman Pavlo Skoropadsky made it his temporary headquarters, and the local people seem to have fallen for it. After all, who wouldn't want to be ruled by a man with such brilliant pair of moustaches.
24 A name I'd prudently rather not decipher.
25 Yuri Shevelov analyzes this phenomenon in detail in his essay, "The Fourth Kharkiv". I highly recommend reading that.

fridges). As a kid, I thought it was just a silly joke. Surely, it was delivered with an awkward smile. I'm not so sure anymore.

Today, in Kursk, the Ukrainian military meet with a similar indifferent response from the locals, who do not feel any power in their own state and don't really care where they live, in Ukraine or Russia, or the Third Reich. The sad thing is, Russian intellectual and opposition figures do not see this very obvious phenomenon — the striking loss of moral identity in their people. Exiled Russian elites feel comfortable being elites, living in the West and upholding a superior existence to that of their compatriots. Such intellectuals cling to their great Russian culture like broke aristocrats clung to their motheaten furs after World War I, carefully avoiding the true Russian culture — the world of moral indifference, of ethical void, where principles and human dignity are set aside, far from their living spaces, like the open-air lavatories they so touchingly install over all the endless Russian territories.

The disaffectedness of the Russian people is fascinating and terrifying, whichever comes first. And though Kharkiv locals might be the best experts on Russian people's behavior, it is still a mystery to me why the citizens of Bilhorod cheered when they saw those missiles flying to kill us. I don't have an explanation for that. I will probably never have one. The only way I could express my obsessive desire to understand the true, not great, Russian culture was through fantasy. And so, in my horror dreams, a dead Russian soldier is forever trying to settle in my apartment and build an Olympic stadium on the site of my school yard, as he did in Sochi on the home of Circassians.

Ukrainians also have an unexplained compartment in their mental structures. This part of our brain is designed to always believe in victory, but in our own, darkly pessimistic way. In Ukrainian, there is an expression of hopelessness, "лягати в помиральну яму" – "to go lie in the dying pit". Instead of a grave we say "the dying pit", literally a hole in the ground where we plan to lie and wait for death to come. Every time a Western country refuses weapons, or Russia launches a brutal attack on a cancer hospital, or videos of executions of our soldiers and civilians by the Russian military surface, we go and lie in our imaginary dying pits and wait for the nukes to finally end it all. Scrolling through another post about the dying pit on Twitter the other day, I came across my favorite piece of Ukrainian optimism so far. It perfectly described Ukrainians' sarcastic hope. "No worries," the author of the reply said, "we will grow a garden in this dying pit".

Living in Kharkiv is like growing a garden in the dying pit. This cheerful repurposing of the dying pit is what makes me believe in Ukraine and its people the most. We, the descendants of farmers and slaves, Scythians and Polovtsian kurgans, can certainly grow a garden in our cozy, recycled, gluten-free dying pits. And we will have oat milk lattes and espresso tonics in our pit. And we will try to make sure there are enough benches and rubbish bins and square Buffet pizzas to allow us to enjoy these gardens in the best city in the world, Kharkiv.

"Why don't you leave?", people ask. The familiar questions have floated in the Ukrainian east ever since this war began in 2014. I could give a billion reasons, economic and political, rational and well-researched, but I feel that a friend of mine provided the perfect explanation, when he said that "at some point you just want to eat with your own forks". And this book is really about how we, the Kharkivians, continue to eat with our own forks, come rain, sun, or North Korean ballistic missiles; and about how we start to think of the history behind these forks. About our families tortured and starved in the previous iterations of empire. Our streets and our names come alive and change, as a zombie monster is trying to devour our fragile, beautiful and ugly living, breathing bodies. And we furnish our dying pits and think and wonder; we will continue to do so for a long time yet.

As for my own optimism (I am involuntarily crying as I write this, by the way), in the third year of the big war I have a flat in central Kharkiv. It is temporarily working as a residence for artists and writers who, despite everything, are inventing new senses of what this city and the whole of the Ukrainian east can become. I've decided to grow a garden in a pretty five-story dying pit. And wait.[26]

We have an old joke about waiting. A Ukrainian tells his friend, "You know, the real winner of World War II was the Ukrainian Insurgent Army". When his friend laughs in disbelief, the man persists, "Tell me, then, what did the Ukrainian insurgents fight for?" "They fought for an independent Ukraine", he says. "Correct, and what did Hitler fight for?" "The Third Reich", he answers. "Yes, and what did Stalin fight for?" "For the Soviet Union", he replies. "Exaclty. So where are the Third Reich and the Soviet Union now?"

This joke has a grain of truth to it. Ukrainians are a patient nation. Unlike the Russians, often described as impulsive, we can wait for a very long time, step by step, methodically approaching our goal. A nation that has never boasted great victories, that has never bathed in the glory of imperial conquest, Ukrainians have grown to be modest and patient. Our fairytales never have a happy ending. A modestly optimistic at best. We have been an extremely unlucky nation. Prior to 1991, we were the biggest ethnic group in the world without its own state. Today Kurdish people hold this distinction. The only bits of luck we had, historically, were carved out of the bleeding bodies of our enemies. We are patient, but not the turn-the-other-cheek pacifist kind of patient. We have sharp teeth and long claws.

In 2021, in Kramatorsk, I visited an exhibition titled *Rebellious Gene* at a local history museum. Organized by the brilliant curator Dmytro Bilko, the exhibition, among other items, displayed *kryivka*, the hiding place of a Ukrainian insurgent army unit on the bank of the Donets River. Insurgents weren't numerous in the Ukrainian east, as the Holodomor and repressions had seriously reduced the will of locals to resist. And yet, there was resistance here even then, the few Insurgent Army rebels fighting for an independent Ukraine in the Wild Field of the 1940s. As Dmytro himself is now doing, having joined the Ukrainian armed forces. In 2023 he delivered a lecture on the cultural anthropology of military selfies from a trench

---

[26] I still need to fix the balcony door, so dying is out of the question for now.

near where he used to conduct an archaeological practice back in the 1990s. The rebellious gene grinds on.

And sometimes history loves such industrious underdogs. Nobody believed that the Third Reich or the Soviet Union would disappear mere days before they did. Nobody believed that Ukraine would become independent (except Ukrainians, of course). Today, likewise, the Russian Federation seems unbreakable; North Korean, Iranian and Syrian dictatorial regimes eternal; while Ukraine is still viewed as an accident, a spelling mistake in a sidenote. Will history smile upon our tired faces, and play another darkly humorous joke on 'realpolitik' Chamberlain-type folks? Will history let our enemies melt "like dew in the sun" as our mildly pessimistic anthem suggests they should? Who knows. We will once again take the risk and see. Like the last Insurgent Army fighters who crawled out of their hiding spots in the Carpathian mountains, sometime in the 1990s, to participate in the second presidential elections of a country they didn't know existed but which they had been fighting for all their lives, preserving it inside their bodies for five decades. Like these patient rebels, we will try to be especially careful to survive and see the sun rise from our clean energy sustainable trendy dying pits.

November 2024

Acknowledgements

I want to thank a huge number of people, but my memory fails, so if you aren't on the list, coffee's on me (the honorarium from this book will surely cover it). On a serious note, I want to thank the brilliant journalist and writer Maksym Eristavi, who, in the most open-hearted way, encouraged me to publish (and whose book *Russian Imperialism 101* should really be on your bedside tables). I'm grateful to Mette High and Emily Finer, who are the kind of scholar I aspire to become, for reading the manuscript in its early stages. I thank Victoria Donovan, who has been the greatest inspiration as both researcher and friend, and whose book, *Life in Spite of Everything*, makes me believe in humanity.

Of course, I'm grateful to my friends, especially "the Karazin University Brothers" Anya Tkachenko and Nastia Dashkova, and Nadya Noskova, who once, on a picnic in Sarzhyn Yar, said to me, "If amoeba made it, we will make it too!" I'm grateful, too, to Vika Ivanova, my partner-in-crime on the road to cinematic success (*Khastoria: Kharkiv Legends* is available on our YouTube channel, if that still exists in the distant future when you read this). Great thanks to Tanya Pukhnavtseva, one of the deepest and most philosophical contemporary artists I know, for visualizing what I've dreamt about for the cover of this book. Thanks to the brilliant Vasylysa and Hjørdis, and to the time when our friendship was forged over another book, *Kharkiv is a Dream*, a dreamy twin to this somber child of mine.

I want to thank my family — my parents, my brother and his wife, and my lovely nieces and nephew. To all the Kharkiv friends met before and after 2022, all those who left and the ones who remain, who moved here, inspired by the energy of this place. For we are the only ones who've had the pleasure of living in the best city in the inhabited universe, of walking the largest square in our galaxy, of eating the blasted pineapple square pizza in Buffet, sitting on the most luxurious benches in human history.

Finally, I want to thank the Ukrainian defenders and all who bring justice closer to home. May you reach your goals, and your road be smooth.

Hugs,
V.

UKRAINIAN VOICES

Collected by Andreas Umland

1   Mychailo Wynnyckyj
    Ukraine's Maidan, Russia's
    War
    A Chronicle and Analysis of the
    Revolution of Dignity
    With a foreword by Serhii
    Plokhy
    ISBN 978-3-8382-1327-9

2   Olexander Hryb
    Understanding
    Contemporary Ukrainian
    and Russian Nationalism
    The Post-Soviet Cossack Revival
    and Ukraine's National Security
    With a foreword by Vitali Vitaliev
    ISBN 978-3-8382-1377-4

3   Marko Bojcun
    Towards a Political Economy
    of Ukraine
    Selected Essays 1990–2015
    With a foreword by John-Paul
    Himka
    ISBN 978-3-8382-1368-2

4   Volodymyr Yermolenko
    (ed.)
    Ukraine in Histories and
    Stories
    Essays by Ukrainian
    Intellectuals
    With a preface by Peter
    Pomerantsev
    ISBN 978-3-8382-1456-6

5   Mykola Riabchuk
    At the Fence of Metternich's
    Garden
    Essays on Europe, Ukraine, and
    Europeanization
    ISBN 978-3-8382-1484-9

6   Marta Dyczok
    Ukraine Calling
    A Kaleidoscope from
    Hromadske Radio 2016–2019
    With a foreword by Andriy
    Kulykov
    ISBN 978-3-8382-1472-6

7   Olexander Scherba
    Ukraine vs. Darkness
    Undiplomatic Thoughts
    With a foreword by Adrian
    Karatnycky
    ISBN 978-3-8382-1501-3

8   Olesya Yaremchuk
    Our Others
    Stories of Ukrainian Diversity
    With a foreword by Ostap
    Slyvynsky
    Translated from the Ukrainian by
    Zenia Tompkins and Hanna Leliv
    ISBN 978-3-8382-1475-7

9   Nataliya Gumenyuk
    Die verlorene Insel
    Geschichten von der besetzten
    Krim
    Mit einem Vorwort von Alice
    Bota
    Aus dem Ukrainischen übersetzt
    von Johann Zajaczkowski
    ISBN 978-3-8382-1499-3

10 Olena Stiazhkina
    Zero Point Ukraine
    Four Essays on World War II
    Translated from the Ukrainian
    by Svitlana Kulinska
    ISBN 978-3-8382-1550-1

11 Oleksii Sinchenko, Dmytro Stus, Leonid Finberg (compilers)
    Ukrainian Dissidents
    An Anthology of Texts
    ISBN 978-3-8382-1551-8

12 John-Paul Himka
    Ukrainian Nationalists and the Holocaust
    OUN and UPA's Participation in the Destruction of Ukrainian Jewry, 1941–1944
    ISBN 978-3-8382-1548-8

13 Andrey Demartino
    False Mirrors
    The Weaponization of Social Media in Russia's Operation to Annex Crimea
    With a foreword by Oleksiy Danilov
    ISBN 978-3-8382-1533-4

14 Svitlana Biedarieva (ed.)
    Contemporary Ukrainian and Baltic Art
    Political and Social Perspectives, 1991–2021
    ISBN 978-3-8382-1526-6

15 Olesya Khromeychuk
    A Loss
    The Story of a Dead Soldier Told by His Sister
    With a foreword by Andrey Kurkov
    ISBN 978-3-8382-1570-9

16 Marieluise Beck (Hg.)
    Ukraine verstehen
    Auf den Spuren von Terror und Gewalt
    Mit einem Vorwort von Dmytro Kuleba
    ISBN 978-3-8382-1653-9

17 Stanislav Aseyev
    Heller Weg
    Geschichte eines Konzentrationslagers im Donbass 2017–2019
    Aus dem Russischen übersetzt von Martina Steis und Charis Haska
    ISBN 978-3-8382-1620-1

18 Mykola Davydiuk
    Wie funktioniert Putins Propaganda?
    Anmerkungen zum Informationskrieg des Kremls
    Aus dem Ukrainischen übersetzt von Christian Weise
    ISBN 978-3-8382-1628-7

19 Olesya Yaremchuk
    Unsere Anderen
    Geschichten ukrainischer Vielfalt
    Aus dem Ukrainischen übersetzt von Christian Weise
    ISBN 978-3-8382-1635-5

20 Oleksandr Mykhed
    „Dein Blut wird die Kohle tränken"
    Über die Ostukraine
    Aus dem Ukrainischen übersetzt von Simon Muschick und Dario Planert
    ISBN 978-3-8382-1648-5

21 Vakhtang Kipiani (Hg.)
    Der Zweite Weltkrieg in der Ukraine
    Geschichte und Lebensgeschichten
    Aus dem Ukrainischen übersetzt von Margarita Grinko
    ISBN 978-3-8382-1622-5

22 Vakhtang Kipiani (ed.)
    World War II, Uncontrived and Unredacted
    Testimonies from Ukraine
    Translated from the Ukrainian by Zenia Tompkins and Daisy Gibbons
    ISBN 978-3-8382-1621-8

23 *Dmytro Stus*
   Vasyl Stus
   Life in Creativity
   Translated from the Ukrainian by
   Ludmila Bachurina
   ISBN 978-3-8382-1631-7

24 *Vitalii Ogiienko (ed.)*
   The Holodomor and the
   Origins of the Soviet Man
   Reading the Testimony of
   Anastasia Lysyvets
   With forewords by Natalka
   Bilotserkivets and Serhy
   Yekelchyk
   Translated from the Ukrainian by
   Alla Parkhomenko and
   Alexander J. Motyl
   ISBN 978-3-8382-1616-4

25 *Vladislav Davidzon*
   Jewish-Ukrainian Relations
   and the Birth of a Political
   Nation
   Selected Writings 2013-2021
   With a foreword by Bernard-
   Henri Lévy
   ISBN 978-3-8382-1509-9

26 *Serhy Yekelchyk*
   Writing the Nation
   The Ukrainian Historical
   Profession in Independent
   Ukraine and the Diaspora
   ISBN 978-3-8382-1695-9

27 *Ildi Eperjesi, Oleksandr Kachura*
   Shreds of War
   Fates from the Donbas Frontline
   2014-2019
   With a foreword by Olexiy
   Haran
   ISBN 978-3-8382-1680-5

28 *Oleksandr Melnyk*
   World War II as an Identity
   Project
   Historicism, Legitimacy
   Contests, and the (Re-)Con-
   struction of Political Commu-
   nities in Ukraine, 1939–1946
   With a foreword by David R.
   Marples
   ISBN 978-3-8382-1704-8

29 *Olesya Khromeychuk*
   Ein Verlust
   Die Geschichte eines gefallenen
   ukrainischen Soldaten, erzählt
   von seiner Schwester
   Mit einem Vorwort von Andrej
   Kurkow
   Aus dem Englischen übersetzt
   von Lily Sophie
   ISBN 978-3-8382-1770-3

30 *Tamara Martsenyuk, Tetiana Kostiuchenko (eds.)*
   Russia's War in Ukraine
   During 2022
   Personal Experiences of
   Ukrainian Scholars
   ISBN 978-3-8382-1757-4

31 *Ildikó Eperjesi, Oleksandr Kachura*
   Shreds of War. Vol. 2
   Fates from Crimea 2015–2022
   With an interview of Oleh
   Sentsov
   ISBN 978-3-8382-1780-2

32 *Yuriy Lukanov*
   The Press
   How Russia Destroyed Media
   Freedom in Crimea
   With a foreword by Taras Kuzio
   ISBN 978-3-8382-1784-0

33 *Megan Buskey*
   Ukraine Is Not Dead Yet
   A Family Story of Exile and
   Return
   ISBN 978-3-8382-1691-1

34 *Vira Ageyeva*
Behind the Scenes of the Empire
Essays on Cultural Relationships between Ukraine and Russia
With a foreword by Oksana Zabuzhko
ISBN 978-3-8382-1748-2

35 *Marieluise Beck (ed.)*
Understanding Ukraine
Tracing the Roots of Terror and Violence
With a foreword by Dmytro Kuleba
ISBN 978-3-8382-1773-4

36 *Olesya Khromeychuk*
A Loss
The Story of a Dead Soldier Told by His Sister, 2nd edn.
With a foreword by Philippe Sands
With a preface by Andrii Kurkov
ISBN 978-3-8382-1870-0

37 *Taras Kuzio, Stefan Jajecznyk-Kelman*
Fascism and Genocide
Russia's War Against Ukrainians
ISBN 978-3-8382-1791-8

38 *Alina Nychyk*
Ukraine Vis-à-Vis Russia and the EU
Misperceptions of Foreign Challenges in Times of War, 2014–2015
With a foreword by Paul D'Anieri
ISBN 978-3-8382-1767-3

39 *Sasha Dovzhyk (ed.)*
Ukraine Lab
Global Security, Environment, and Disinformation Through the Prism of Ukraine
With a foreword by Rory Finnin
ISBN 978-3-8382-1805-2

40 *Serhiy Kvit*
Media, History, and Education
Three Ways to Ukrainian Independence
With a preface by Diane Francis
ISBN 978-3-8382-1807-6

41 *Anna Romandash*
Women of Ukraine
Reportages from the War and Beyond
ISBN 978-3-8382-1819-9

42 *Dominika Rank*
Matzewe in meinem Garten
Abenteuer eines jüdischen Heritage-Touristen in der Ukraine
ISBN 978-3-8382-1810-6

43 *Myroslaw Marynowytsch*
Das Universum hinter dem Stacheldraht
Memoiren eines sowjet-ukrainischen Dissidenten
Mit einem Vorwort von Timothy Snyder und einem Nachwort von Max Hartmann
ISBN 978-3-8382-1806-9

44 *Konstantin Sigow*
Für Deine und meine Freiheit
Europäische Revolutions- und Kriegserfahrungen im heutigen Kyjiw
Mit einem Vorwort von Karl Schlögel
Herausgegeben von Regula M. Zwahlen
ISBN 978-3-8382-1755-0

45 *Kateryna Pylypchuk*
The War that Changed Us
Ukrainian Novellas, Poems, and Essays from 2022
With a foreword by Victor Yushchenko
Paperback
ISBN 978-3-8382-1859-5
Hardcover
ISBN 978-3-8382-1860-1

46 Kyrylo Tkachenko
    Rechte Tür Links
    Radikale Linke in Deutschland,
    die Revolution und der Krieg in
    der Ukraine, 2013-2018
    ISBN 978-3-8382-1711-6

47 Alexander Strashny
    The Ukrainian Mentality
    An Ethno-Psychological,
    Historical and Comparative
    Exploration
    With a foreword by Antonina
    Lovochkina
    Translated from the Ukrainian
    by Michael M. Naydan and
    Olha Tytarenko
    ISBN 978-3-8382-1886-1

48 Alona Shestopalova
    From Screens to Battlefields
    Tracing the Construction of
    Enemies on Russian Television
    With a foreword by Nina
    Jankowicz
    ISBN 978-3-8382-1884-7

49 Iaroslav Petik
    Politics and Society in the
    Ukrainian People's Republic
    (1917–1921) and
    Contemporary Ukraine
    (2013–2022)
    A Comparative Analysis
    With a foreword by Mykola
    Doroshko
    ISBN 978-3-8382-1817-5

50 Serhii Plokhy
    Der Mann mit der
    Giftpistole
    Eine Spionagageschichte aus dem
    Kalten Krieg
    ISBN 978-3-8382-1789-5

51 Vakhtang Kipiani
    Ukrainische Dissidenten
    unter der Sowjetmacht
    Im Kampf um Wahrheit und
    Freiheit
    Aus dem Ukrainischen übersetzt
    von Christian Weise
    ISBN 978-3-8382-1890-8

52 Dmytro Shestakov
    When Businesses Test
    Hypotheses
    A Four-Step Approach to Risk
    Management for Innovative
    Startups
    With a foreword by Anthony J.
    Tether
    ISBN 978-3-8382-1883-0

53 Larissa Babij
    A Kind of Refugee
    The Story of an American Who
    Refused to Leave Ukraine
    With a foreword by Vladislav
    Davidzon
    ISBN 978-3-8382-1898-4

54 Julia Davis
    In Their Own Words
    How Russian Propagandists
    Reveal Putin's Intentions
    With a foreword by Timothy
    Snyder
    ISBN 978-3-8382-1909-7

55 Sonya Atlantova, Oleksandr
    Klymenko
    Icons on Ammo Boxes
    Painting Life on the Remnants of
    Russia's War in Donbas, 2014-21
    Translated from the Ukrainian by
    Anastasya Knyazhytska
    ISBN 978-3-8382-1892-2

56 Leonid Ushkalov
    Catching an Elusive Bird
    The Life of Hryhorii Skovoroda
    Translated from the Ukrainian
    by Natalia Komarova
    ISBN 978-3-8382-1894-6

57 Vakhtang Kipiani
    Ein Land weiblichen
    Geschlechts
    Ukrainische Frauenschicksale
    im 20. und 21. Jahrhundert
    Aus dem Ukrainischen übersetzt
    von Christian Weise
    ISBN 978-3-8382-1891-5

58 Petro Rychlo
„Zerrissne Saiten einer
überlauten Harfe ..."
Deutschjüdische Dichter der
Bukowina
ISBN 978-3-8382-1893-9

59 Volodymyr Paniotto
Sociology in Jokes
An Entertaining Introduction
ISBN 978-3-8382-1857-1

60 Josef Wallmannsberger
(ed.)
Executing Renaissances
The Poetological Nation of
Ukraine
ISBN 978-3-8382-1741-3

61 Pavlo Kazarin
The Wild West of Eastern
Europe
A Ukrainian Guide on Breaking
Free from Empire
Translated from the Ukrainian
by Dominique Hoffman
ISBN 978-3-8382-1842-7

62 Ernest Gyidel
Ukrainian Public
Nationalism in the General
Government
The Case of *Krakivski Visti*,
1940–1944
With a foreword by David R.
Marples
ISBN 978-3-8382-1865-6

63 Olexander Hryb
Understanding
Contemporary Russian
Militarism
From Revolutionary to New
Generation Warfare
With a foreword by Mark Laity
ISBN 978-3-8382-1927-1

64 Orysia Hrudka, Bohdan Ben
Dark Days, Determined
People
Stories from Ukraine under Siege
With a foreword by Myroslav
Marynovych
ISBN 978-3-8382-1958-5

65 Oleksandr Pankieiev (ed.)
Narratives of the Russo-
Ukrainian War
A Look Within and Without
With a foreword by Natalia
Khanenko-Friesen
ISBN 978-3-8382-1964-6

66 Roman Sohn, Ariana Gic
(eds.)
Unrecognized War
The Fight for Truth about
Russia's War on Ukraine
With a foreword by Viktor
Yushchenko
ISBN 978-3-8382-1947-9

67 Paul Robert Magocsi
Ukraina Redux
Schon wieder die Ukraine ...
ISBN 978-3-8382-1942-4

68 Paul Robert Magocsi
L'Ucraina Ritrovata
Sullo Stato e l'Identità Nazionale
ISBN 978-3-8382-1982-0

69 Max Hartmann
Ein Schrei der Verzweiflung
Aquarelle von Danylo Movchan
zu Russlands Krieg in der
Ukraine
Mit einem Vorwort von Mateusz
Sora
Paperback
ISBN 978-3-8382-2011-6
Hardcover
ISBN 978-3-8382-2012-3

70 Vakhtang Kebuladze (Hg.)
Die Zukunft, die wir uns
wünschen
Essays aus der Ukraine
ISBN 978-3-8382-1531-0

71 Marieluise Beck, Jan Claas Behrends, Gelinada Grinchenko und Oksana Mikheieva (Hgg.)
Deutsch-ukrainische Geschichten
Bruchstücke aus einer gemeinsamen Vergangenheit
ISBN 978-3-8382-2053-6

72 Pavlo Kazarin
Der Wilde Westen Ost-Europas
Der ukrainische Weg aus dem Imperium
Aus dem Ukrainischen übersetzt von Christian Weise
ISBN 978-3-8382-1843-4

73 Radomyr Mokryk
Die ukrainischen »Sechziger«
Chronologie einer Revolte
ISBN 978-3-8382-1873-1

74 Leonid Finberg
My Ukraine
Rethinking the Past, Building the Present
ISBN 978-3-8382-1974-5

75 Joseph Zissels
Consider My Inmost Thoughts
Essays, Lectures, and Interviews on Ukrainian Matters at the Turn of the Century
ISBN 978-3-8382-1975-2

76 Margarita Yehorchenko, Iryna Berlyand, Ihor Vinokurov (eds.)
Jewish Addresses in Ukraine
A Guide-Book
With a foreword by Leonid Finberg
ISB 978-3-8382-1976-9

77 Viktoriia Grivina
Kharkiv—A War City
A Collection of Essays from 2022–23
ISBN 978-3-8382-1988-2

78 Hjørdis Clemmensen, Viktoriia Grivina, Vasylysa Shchogoleva
Kharkiv Is a Dream
Public Art and Activism 2013–2023
With a foreword by Bohdan Volynskyi
ISBN 978-3-8382-2005-5

79 Olga Khomenko
The Faraway Sky of Kyiv
Ukrainians in the War
With a foreword by Hiroaki Kuromiya
ISBN 978-3-8382-2006-2

80 Daria Mattingly, Jonathon Vsetecka (eds.)
The Holodomor in Global Perspective
How the Famine in Ukraine Shaped the World
With a foreword by Anne Applebaum
ISBN 978-3-8382-1953-0

81 Olga Khomenko
Ukrainians beyond Borders
Nine Life Journeys Through the History of Eastern Europe
With a foreword by Zbigniew Wojnowski
ISBN 978-3-8382-2007-9

82 Mykhailo Minakov
From Servant to Leader
Chronicles of Ukraine under the Zelensky Presidency, 2019–2024
With a foreword by John Lloyd
ISBN 978-3-8382-2002-4

83 Volodymyr Hromov (ed.)
A Ruined Home
Sketches of War, 2022–2023
ISBN 978-3-8382-2008-6

84 *Olha Tatokhina (Ed.)*
   Why Do They Kill Our People?
   Russia's War Against Ukraine as
   Told by Ukrainians
   With a foreword by Volodymyr
   Yermolenko
   ISBN 978-3-8382-2056-7

85 *Mieste Hotopp-Riecke,
   Sarah Reinke (Hrsg.)*
   Die Krimtataren
   Geschichte – Kultur – Politik
   Mit einem Vorwort von
   Nariman Dschelal
   ISBN 978-3-8382-1986-8

86 *Max Hartmann (ed.)*
   A Cry of Despair
   Danylo Movchan's Watercolors
   on the War in Ukraine
   With a foreword by John A.
   Kohan and Matheusz Sora
   ISBN 978-3-8382-2051-2

87 *Olha Marmilova, Yuliia
   Soroka (eds.)*
   **The Russian War Against
   Ukraine**
   Investigations of Its Social and
   Historical Context, 2014–2024
   With a foreword by Ulrich
   Schmid
   ISBN 978-3-8382-2035-2

88 *Mykola Davidyuk*
   **How Putin's Propaganda
   Works**
   Ukraine's Experience in Its War
   Against Russia since 2014
   With a foreword by Roman
   Kostenko
   ISBN 978-3-8382-1627-0

89 *Mikhail Minakov*
   Der postsowjetische Mensch
   Philosophische Betrachtungen
   zur Gesellschaftsgeschichte nach
   Ende der UdSSR
   Mit einem Vorwort von Timm
   Beichelt
   Aus dem Englischen übersetzt
   von Hermann Haushahn
   ISBN 978-3-8382-2043-7

Book series "Ukrainian Voices"

Coordinator
Andreas Umland, National University of Kyiv-Mohyla Academy

Editorial Board
Lesia Bidochko, National University of Kyiv-Mohyla Academy
Svitlana Biedarieva, George Washington University, DC, USA
Ivan Gomza, Kyiv School of Economics, Ukraine
Natalie Jaresko, Aspen Institute, Kyiv/Washington
Olena Lennon, University of New Haven, West Haven, USA
Kateryna Yushchenko, First Lady of Ukraine 2005-2010, Kyiv
Oleksandr Zabirko, University of Regensburg, Germany

Advisory Board
Iuliia Bentia, National Academy of Arts of Ukraine, Kyiv
Natalya Belitser, Pylyp Orlyk Institute for Democracy, Kyiv
Oleksandra Bienert, Humboldt University of Berlin, Germany
Sergiy Bilenky, Canadian Institute of Ukrainian Studies, Toronto
Tymofii Brik, Kyiv School of Economics, Ukraine
Olga Brusylovska, Mechnikov National University, Odesa
Mariana Budjeryn, Harvard University, Cambridge, USA
Volodymyr Bugrov, Shevchenko National University, Kyiv
Olga Burlyuk, University of Amsterdam, The Netherlands
Yevhen Bystrytsky, NAS Institute of Philosophy, Kyiv
Andrii Danylenko, Pace University, New York, USA
Vladislav Davidzon, Atlantic Council, Washington/Paris
Mykola Davydiuk, Think Tank "Polityka," Kyiv
Andrii Demartino, National Security and Defense Council, Kyiv
Vadym Denisenko, Ukrainian Institute for the Future, Kyiv
Oleksandr Donii, Center for Political Values Studies, Kyiv
Volodymyr Dubovyk, Mechnikov National University, Odesa
Volodymyr Dubrovskiy, CASE Ukraine, Kyiv
Diana Dutsyk, National University of Kyiv-Mohyla Academy
Marta Dyczok, Western University, Ontario, Canada
Yevhen Fedchenko, National University of Kyiv-Mohyla Academy
Sofiya Filonenko, State Pedagogical University of Berdyansk
Oleksandr Fisun, Karazin National University, Kharkiv
Oksana Forostyna, Webjournal "Ukraina Moderna," Kyiv
Roman Goncharenko, Broadcaster "Deutsche Welle," Bonn
George Grabowicz, Harvard University, Cambridge, USA
Gelinada Grinchenko, Karazin National University, Kharkiv
Kateryna Härtel, Federal Union of European Nationalities, Brussels
Nataliia Hendel, University of Geneva, Switzerland
Anton Herashchenko, Kyiv School of Public Administration
John-Paul Himka, University of Alberta, Edmonton
Ola Hnatiuk, National University of Kyiv-Mohyla Academy
Oleksandr Holubov, Broadcaster "Deutsche Welle," Bonn
Yaroslav Hrytsak, Ukrainian Catholic University, Lviv
Oleksandra Humenna, National University of Kyiv-Mohyla Academy
Tamara Hundorova, NAS Institute of Literature, Kyiv
Oksana Huss, University of Bologna, Italy
Oleksandra Iwaniuk, University of Warsaw, Poland
Mykola Kapitonenko, Shevchenko National University, Kyiv
Georgiy Kasianov, Marie Curie-Skłodowska University, Lublin
Vakhtang Kebuladze, Shevchenko National University, Kyiv
Natalia Khanenko-Friesen, University of Alberta, Edmonton
Victoria Khiterer, Millersville University of Pennsylvania, USA
Oksana Kis, NAS Institute of Ethnology, Lviv
Pavlo Klimkin, Center for National Resilience and Development, Kyiv
Oleksandra Kolomiiets, Center for Economic Strategy, Kyiv

Sergiy Korsunsky, Kobe Gakuin University, Japan
Nadiia Koval, Kyiv School of Economics, Ukraine
Volodymyr Kravchenko, University of Alberta, Edmonton
Oleksiy Kresin, NAS Koretskiy Institute of State and Law, Kyiv
Anatoliy Kruglashov, Fedkovych National University, Chernivtsi
Andrey Kurkov, PEN Ukraine, Kyiv
Ostap Kushnir, Lazarski University, Warsaw
Taras Kuzio, National University of Kyiv-Mohyla Academy
Serhii Kvit, National University of Kyiv-Mohyla Academy
Yuliya Ladygina, The Pennsylvania State University, USA
Yevhen Mahda, Institute of World Policy, Kyiv
Victoria Malko, California State University, Fresno, USA
Yulia Marushevska, Security and Defense Center (SAND), Kyiv
Myroslav Marynovych, Ukrainian Catholic University, Lviv
Oleksandra Matviichuk, Center for Civil Liberties, Kyiv
Mykhailo Minakov, Kennan Institute, Washington, USA
Anton Moiseienko, The Australian National University, Canberra
Alexander Motyl, Rutgers University-Newark, USA
Vlad Mykhnenko, University of Oxford, United Kingdom
Vitalii Ogiienko, Ukrainian Institute of National Remembrance, Kyiv
Olga Onuch, University of Manchester, United Kingdom
Olesya Ostrovska, Museum "Mystetskyi Arsenal," Kyiv
Anna Osypchuk, National University of Kyiv-Mohyla Academy
Oleksandr Pankieiev, University of Alberta, Edmonton
Oleksiy Panych, Publishing House "Dukh i Litera," Kyiv
Valerii Pekar, Kyiv-Mohyla Business School, Ukraine
Yohanan Petrovsky-Shtern, Northwestern University, Chicago
Serhii Plokhy, Harvard University, Cambridge, USA
Andrii Portnov, Viadrina University, Frankfurt-Oder, Germany
Maryna Rabinovych, Kyiv School of Economics, Ukraine
Valentyna Romanova, Institute of Developing Economies, Tokyo
Natalya Ryabinska, Collegium Civitas, Warsaw, Poland
Darya Tsymbalyk, University of Oxford, United Kingdom
Vsevolod Samokhvalov, University of Liege, Belgium
Orest Semotiuk, Franko National University, Lviv
Viktoriya Sereda, NAS Institute of Ethnology, Lviv
Anton Shekhovtsov, University of Vienna, Austria
Andriy Shevchenko, Media Center Ukraine, Kyiv
Oxana Shevel, Tufts University, Medford, USA
Pavlo Shopin, National Pedagogical Dragomanov University, Kyiv
Karina Shyrokykh, Stockholm University, Sweden
Nadja Simon, freelance interpreter, Cologne, Germany
Olena Snigova, NAS Institute for Economics and Forecasting, Kyiv
Ilona Solohub, Analytical Platform "VoxUkraine," Kyiv
Iryna Solonenko, LibMod - Center for Liberal Modernity, Berlin
Galyna Solovei, National University of Kyiv-Mohyla Academy
Sergiy Stelmakh, NAS Institute of World History, Kyiv
Olena Stiazhkina, NAS Institute of the History of Ukraine, Kyiv
Dmitri Stratievski, Osteuropa Zentrum (OEZB), Berlin
Dmytro Stus, National Taras Shevchenko Museum, Kyiv
Frank Sysyn, University of Toronto, Canada
Olha Tokariuk, Center for European Policy Analysis, Washington
Olena Tregub, Independent Anti-Corruption Commission, Kyiv
Hlib Vyshlinsky, Centre for Economic Strategy, Kyiv
Mychailo Wynnyckyj, National University of Kyiv-Mohyla Academy
Yelyzaveta Yasko, NGO "Yellow Blue Strategy," Kyiv
Serhy Yekelchyk, University of Victoria, Canada
Victor Yushchenko, President of Ukraine 2005-2010, Kyiv
Oleksandr Zaitsev, Ukrainian Catholic University, Lviv
Kateryna Zarembo, National University of Kyiv-Mohyla Academy
Yaroslav Zhalilo, National Institute for Strategic Studies, Kyiv
Sergei Zhuk, Ball State University at Muncie, USA
Alina Zubkovych, Nordic Ukraine Forum, Stockholm
Liudmyla Zubrytska, National University of Kyiv-Mohyla Academy

Friends of the Series

Ana Maria Abulescu, University of Bucharest, Romania
Łukasz Adamski, Centrum Mieroszewskiego, Warsaw
Marieluise Beck, LibMod—Center for Liberal Modernity, Berlin
Marc Berensen, King's College London, United Kingdom
Johannes Bohnen, BOHNEN Public Affairs, Berlin
Karsten Brüggemann, University of Tallinn, Estonia
Ulf Brunnbauer, Leibniz Institute (IOS), Regensburg
Martin Dietze, German-Ukrainian Culture Society, Hamburg
Gergana Dimova, Florida State University, Tallahassee/London
Caroline von Gall, Goethe University, Frankfurt-Main
Zaur Gasimov, Rhenish Friedrich Wilhelm University, Bonn
Armand Gosu, University of Bucharest, Romania
Thomas Grant, University of Cambridge, United Kingdom
Gustav Gressel, European Council on Foreign Relations, Berlin
Rebecca Harms, European Centre for Press & Media Freedom, Leipzig
André Härtel, Stiftung Wissenschaft und Politik, Berlin/Brussels
Marcel Van Herpen, The Cicero Foundation, Maastricht
Richard Herzinger, freelance analyst, Berlin
Mieste Hotopp-Riecke, ICATAT, Magdeburg
Nico Lange, Munich Security Conference, Berlin
Martin Malek, freelance analyst, Vienna
Ingo Mannteufel, Broadcaster "Deutsche Welle," Bonn
Carlo Masala, Bundeswehr University, Munich
Wolfgang Mueller, University of Vienna, Austria
Dietmar Neutatz, Albert Ludwigs University, Freiburg
Torsten Oppelland, Friedrich Schiller University, Jena
Niccolò Pianciola, University of Padua, Italy
Gerald Praschl, German-Ukrainian Forum (DUF), Berlin
Felix Riefer, Think Tank Ideenagentur-Ost, Düsseldorf
Stefan Rohdewald, University of Leipzig, Germany
Sebastian Schäffer, Institute for the Danube Region (IDM), Vienna
Felix Schimansky-Geier, Friedrich Schiller University, Jena
Ulrich Schneckener, University of Osnabrück, Germany
Winfried Schneider-Deters, freelance analyst, Heidelberg/Kyiv
Gerhard Simon, University of Cologne, Germany
Kai Struve, Martin Luther University, Halle/Wittenberg
David Stulik, European Values Center for Security Policy, Prague
Andrzej Szeptycki, University of Warsaw, Poland
Philipp Ther, University of Vienna, Austria
Stefan Troebst, University of Leipzig, Germany

[Please send requests for changes in, corrections of, and additions to, this list to andreas.umland@stanforalumni.org.]

ibidem.eu